IN RE COOPERMAN

Third Edition

Professional Responsibility

D1611475

IN RE COOPERMAN

Third Edition

Professional Responsibility

Anthony J. Bocchino
Feinberg Professor of Litigation Emeritus
Temple University School of Law

NATIONAL INSTITUTE FOR TRIAL ADVOCACY

Address inquiries to:
Reprint Permission
National Institute for Trial Advocacy
1685 38th Street, Suite 200
Boulder, CO 80301-2735
Phone: (800) 225-6482
Fax: (720) 890-7069
E-mail: permissions@nita.org

ISBN 978-1-60156-805-2
eISBN 978-1-60156-806-9

FBA 1805

Printed in the United States of America

SUSTAINABLE FORESTRY INITIATIVE

Certified Chain of Custody
Promoting Sustainable Forestry

www.sfiprogram.org
SFI-01347

 Wolters Kluwer

Official co-publisher of NITA.
WKLegaledu.com/NITA

CONTENTS

ACKNOWLEDGEMENTS

This case file was one of three such files that formed the basis for a course that integrated trial advocacy and the teaching of legal ethics and professionalism that was taught at the Temple University Beasley School of Law that won the 1993 Gambrell Award for training in professionalism from the ABA, the first law school to win this award. The course was designed by myself and my friend and colleague of over thirty-five years, Louis Natali, and I acknowledge his insight, professionalism and friendship.

DEDICATION

To my brother-in-law, Joe Lewis. Ethical, generous, accomplished and one of the very best men I have the privilege of knowing.

INTRODUCTION

This is a four count disciplinary action brought by the Nita State Bar against the respondent, Harriet Cooperman, a member of the Nita State Bar. Count I avers that respondent failed to adequately consult with her client, David Engels, so as to enable him to make informed decisions as to the course of his cause of action against the Acme Paper Company. Count II avers that the respondent failed to adequately explain the contents of her fee agreement with her client. Count III avers that the respondent engaged in the simultaneous representation of clients with conflicting interests without first obtaining the informed consent of her clients to do so. Count IV avers that the respondent engaged in the representation of a client against a former client in a cause of action that was substantially related to the representation of the former client.

Witnesses for the State Bar:

1. David Engels

2. Jamie Doran

3. Nour Basara

Witnesses for the Respondent, Harriet Cooperman:

1. Harriet Cooperman

2. Pat Simpson

3. Cosme Gallo

With the exception of David Engels and Harriet Cooperman, all witnesses are written to be played by a person of any gender or ethnic background.

The State Bar disciplinary procedure provides for full discovery, including the taking of depositions. Charged attorneys are not required to give a deposition, but may do so if they desire. The materials provided herein are the result of the discovery process in the *In Re Cooperman* case.

The Nita State Bar has adopted, in full, the ABA Model Rules of Professional Conduct and references in the complaint are to that document. The relevant portions of the Model Rules are reproduced in the appendix to this case file.

Nita State Bar disciplinary hearings are conducted pursuant to the Federal Rules of Evidence, which have been adopted in full by the State of Nita. The hearing is presided over by a hearing officer who rules on all evidentiary matters. A written decision as to all disciplinary charges is rendered by the Nita State Bar Disciplinary Board, which hears all the evidence presented at the disciplinary hearing.

References to dates in this case file are accomplished in the following manner.

YR-0 is the year in which the hearing is held.

YR-1 is the next preceding year.

YR-2 is the second preceding year, etc.

Assume that the depositions contain all material information that each witness knows. If questions exceed the scope of the depositions, the witness should answer, "I don't know."

SPECIAL INSTRUCTIONS FOR USE AS A FULL TRIAL

When this case file is used as the basis for a full trial, the following witnesses may be called by the parties:

Petitioner:

1. David Engels

2. Jamie Doran

3. Nour Basara

Respondent:

1. Harriet Cooperman

2. Pat Simpson

3. Cosme Gallo

A party need not call all the listed witnesses. Any or all of the witnesses can be called by either party. However, if the opposing party calls a witness, the party for whom the witness is listed may prepare the witness. In this eventuality assume the witness has refused to be prepared by the calling party.

IN THE NITA STATE DISCIPLINARY BOARD
IN AND FOR THE COUNTY OF DARROW
STATE OF NITA

IN RE HARRIET COOPERMAN,	)	DISCIPLINARY HEARING
Respondent	)	YR-1-2145
	)	
	)	
NITA STATE BAR,	)	COMPLAINT
Petitioner	)	

COUNT I

The State Bar charges that Respondent, a licensed practitioner, in the representation of David Engels, during the period of September, YR-3 through October, YR-1, violated Rules 1.2 and 1.4 by failing to adequately communicate with her client in order to enable her client to make informed decisions as to the conduct of his cause of action against the Acme Paper Company.

COUNT II

The State Bar charges that Respondent, a licensed practitioner, in the representation of David Engels, during the period of September, YR-3 through October, YR-l, violated Rule 1.5 by:

    a. failing to adequately explain the contents of her fee agreement with her client; and

    b. failing to state the terms of the fee agreement with sufficient specificity.

COUNT III

The State Bar charges that Respondent, a licensed practitioner, in the representation of David Engels, during the period of September, YR-3 through October, YR-l, violated Rule 1.7 by:

    a. simultaneously representing two clients with conflicting interests; and

    b. engaging in the representation of her client in such a manner as to create a conflict of interest between herself and her client.

COUNT IV

The State Bar charges that Respondent, a licensed practitioner, during the representation of David Engels, during the period of September, YR-3 through October, YR-1, violated Rules 1.9 and 1.10 by representing her client in a cause of action against a former client, Acme Paper Company, such cause of action which was substantially related to the representation of the former client.

The Respondent is hereby called before the Disciplinary Board of the State Bar of Nita to answer to the above stated charges.

NITA STATE DISCIPLINARY BOARD

By: *Marion Carter*

MARION CARTER, Chair
Nita State Disciplinary Board
Nita State Bar Association

December 27, YR-1

DEPOSITIONS

DEPOSITION OF PAT SIMPSON*

My name is Pat Simpson and I live at 7108 Green Street in Nita City. I am twenty-six years old and work as a paralegal at Cooperman & Jones at 1201 Market Street in Nita City. I am also an evening law student at Nita University School of Law where I am in the second year of a four year program. I have been working at Cooperman & Jones for four years, since I graduated with a BA in Political Science from Nita State University in YR-4. With the exception of my four years at Nita State I am a lifelong resident of Nita City. I attended the public schools here. My address is my parents' home. I live there to save on expenses while attending law school. My salary at C & J is $38,000 per year plus an average two- to three-thousand-dollar bonus at the end of the year.

C & J is a twenty person general practice firm. There are seven partners, thirteen associates, and ten paralegals working at the firm. I work solely in the civil litigation section of the firm, which has four partners, seven associates, and five paralegals. Since joining the firm in YR-4, I have worked almost exclusively for the senior partner, Harriet Cooperman. She trained me and over the years we have developed a good working relationship. I consider Ms. Cooperman my mentor. It was Harriet who encouraged me to apply to law school and I hope that when I complete my legal studies that I can go to work as an associate with the firm.

Ms. Cooperman has a plaintiff's personal injury and professional (medical and legal) negligence practice. One of my duties at the firm is to conduct preliminary interviews with potential clients to ascertain the general nature of their case. I also determine whether any potential conflicts of interest exist between current and potential clients or between multiple potential clients, in cases with more than one party involved. We keep a computer record of all current clients at the firm for this purpose. Since the end of January of YR-0 the system has a listing of former clients (for five years after the end of our representation) but that wasn't the case in YR-3 when the events involved here began. When I interviewed Mr. Engels there was no easy way to check potential conflicts with clients that arose from representation that was over five years old. In the old system, the database was refreshed each year to reflect only the past five years of litigation. I understand that the decision for five year retention was based on Nita's four year statute of limitations for contracts, with a one year cushion to account for late filings by a former contract partner. In January the policy changed. We got a lecture about conflicts with previous clients where there is a substantial relationship between the former representation and the proposed representation. Our computer system was modified so that we can check whether there is a potential conflict with a former client. Now we search to see if the firm has represented any potential defendant in a past case. If so we have to pull the case to see if the facts of the former case have anything to do with our potential current case. At any rate, we are to note the previous representation to the partner on the case, along with the information about it and the partner will decide whether a conflict precludes us from taking the case. If the partner

---

* The transcript of Pat Simpson's deposition was excerpted so that only the answers are reprinted here. Assume that this is a true and accurate rendering of those answers.

decides the previous representation should not prevent the firm from signing the client, the partner informs the potential client about the previous representation and explains that their fee agreement will include an acknowledgment of the previous representation and a waiver. If they want to go forward, we use a contingency fee form that shows that waiver. (See EXHIBIT 8.)

The preliminary interview and conflict check is important, especially in the relatively common situation where we are approached by a driver and a passenger of a car who have been involved in a car accident. There is a conflict between the passenger and the driver. The passenger has a cause of action against the driver, and if the passenger sued the driver and the other party involved, the passenger would be virtually guaranteed to receive all of their damages. If the passenger and driver join as co-plaintiffs against another defendant, the passenger's award may be reduced by the percentage of the driver's negligence. Of course if the other party is 100 percent negligent then both the driver and passenger get their full damages. In situations such as this, the firm's policy is to explain the conflict of interest to the potential clients. The firm prefers to represent only one of the parties, but we will represent both the driver and the passenger if they choose to waive the conflict. Even though I do my best to explain the conflict of interest, Ms. Cooperman also explains the potential conflict herself. She has done it so many times, she has virtually memorized the advice and it is always the same. Her explanation always ends with advice that we can take one of the people involved and the other can seek separate counsel. In that case, if we represent the passenger and the driver seeks separate counsel we will sue the driver as well as the other party.

I have a standard procedure for handling these preliminary interviews that I always use. This procedure has been in effect since I joined the firm and began working for Ms. Cooperman and was in effect when I interviewed Mr. Engles and Ms. Rubin. The procedure is as follows:

1) I introduce myself as a paralegal with the firm.

2) I obtain the name and address of the potential client(s).

3) I find out the general nature of the legal problem involved (e.g., car accident, slip and fall, medical negligence, etc.).

4) I find out the date of the incident in question.

5) I find out the names and addresses of other people involved in the incident in question.

6) I check our computer records to ascertain if the firm currently represents potential defendants.

7) Starting this month, we now check our files for former clients as well and our conflict database has grown significantly. Ms. Cooperman is notified regarding former clients (with a brief description of the nature of the case) before she counsels the potential new client.

8) If there is a conflict between a driver and passenger, I explain the conflict and the rights of the passenger to sue the driver. Since this month I also inform them of a potential conflict with a former client, but I leave it to Ms. Cooperman to make the decision whether she believes a conflict exists.

9) If no conflicts exist, I take the potential client in to see Ms. Cooperman. She conducts her own, in-depth, factual interview, and covers again the potential conflict of interest; I normally sit in on the meeting and take notes.

If a conflict of interest exists with a current client (at the time of this case, now former clients are considered as well), I inform Ms. Cooperman of the conflict. She then explains to the potential client that the professional responsibility rules will not allow us to represent them. This procedure usually leaves the potential client disappointed but impressed with the ethical way that the law firm operates.

In the situation where two potential clients who were driver and passenger in a car wreck seek to have us represent both of them, my duties are more complicated. I explain to the two people, who are usually friends or family, that the passenger has a potential claim against the driver and that unless they both agree, the firm cannot represent both of them. Most people in this situation want to have one lawyer represent both potential clients, but if there is any hesitation on their part, Ms. Cooperman will interview the passenger alone and explain the potential lawsuit against the driver (in the typical case, the driver (if liable) will not have any personal liability, damages being paid by insurance) after hearing the details of the case. At that point, the passenger can decide whether to waive the conflict of interest.

In cases where the clients with the potential conflict choose to waive the conflict, this waiver is incorporated into the fee agreement that they sign. Ms. Cooperman always goes over again the significance of the waiver of the conflict with the potential clients before they sign the fee agreement. Since this lawsuit, our records allow us to identify potential conflicts with former clients if the former matter involves substantially the same or similar facts, which would require a waiver from the former client as well.

In September of YR-3, I was the paralegal who conducted the preliminary interview of David Engels and Mary Rubin. As I recall, they were involved in a car accident in January of YR-4, in which they were both injured. After I obtained the preliminary information about them, (names, addresses, the fact it was a car accident case, and the name of the potential defendant) I ascertained that C & J did not currently represent the potential defendant in the case, the Acme Paper Company, whose truck was involved in the accident.

I then followed my then existing standard procedure and explained the potential lawsuit that Mr. Engels, the passenger, had for his injuries against Ms. Rubin, the driver. They seemed surprised at this information but immediately both of them said that they wanted to have the same lawyer because they felt that the accident was the fault of the truck driver. Of course, I had no way of evaluating their claim that the potential defendant was at fault because I had not gone into the specifics of the accident with them. When I offered Mr. Engels the opportunity to be interviewed separately by Ms. Cooperman, he declined. I explained that they would have to sign a waiver, which they agreed to do. I then explained the situation to Ms. Cooperman and brought the clients into her office.

Ms. Cooperman confirmed that Mr. Engels and Ms. Rubin understood the potential conflict of interest and that they agreed to waive the conflict. I'm sure that she did so because they both signed a contingent fee agreement that includes a clear statement of the waiver (See Exhibit 4) and Ms. Cooperman always goes over the conflict issue before asking the client to sign the waiver.

I also sat in on Ms. Cooperman's interview of Mr. Engels and Ms. Rubin. Their case was fairly routine. Ms. Rubin was traveling north on Broad Street when the Acme Paper Company truck turned left onto Montgomery Avenue in front of her. She told us that she was somewhat distracted by a demonstration that was taking place on the corner of Broad and Montgomery and that when she looked back, the truck was turning in front of her. That's when the collision happened. Ms. Rubin received a soft tissue injury to her back and neck (whiplash). She had about $6,000 worth of medical bills and missed work as a school teacher for one week. Mr. Engels was more severely injured. He broke his hip and his arm and had medical expenses of approximately $32,000. He also missed two months of work as a school teacher.

We filed suit in behalf of both Mr. Engels and Ms. Rubin. I did a lot of the paper work on this case and handled countless calls from both Ms. Rubin and Mr. Engels. Even though they were told that it would take at least two years to get a trial date they were constantly calling for Ms. Cooperman. I always returned their calls for her, usually to tell them that nothing was happening. Even though I tried to be helpful and understanding, both of these clients were particularly troublesome. Ms. Rubin was quite rude and Mr. Engels seemed to always need his hand held.

The cases settled in October of YR-1. Mr. Engels' case settled for $70,000 and Ms. Rubin's case settled for $16,000. I'm sure that their cases settled a little low because they both came across poorly at the deposition. I remember that after the depositions, Ms. Cooperman told me that Mr. Engels came across as frightened the entire time the deposition was going on and that Ms. Rubin was apparently as rude in the deposition as she was on the phone with me.

I did not participate in the negotiations in this case but I called both Mr. Engels and Ms. Rubin in late September or early October, YR-1, at Ms. Cooperman's request, to ask them to come in to discuss their case before Ms. Cooperman attempted to reach a settlement. About a week later I again called them to inform them that the defendant had made an offer that Ms. Cooperman wanted to talk with them about. I know that both clients were upset with the settlement amounts and that Mr. Engels has claimed that in the initial meeting with Ms. Cooperman that he was led to believe that his case was worth more. I was at the initial meeting and know that no promises on settlement amount were made by anyone. If Ms. Cooperman felt that the cases were worth more, I'm sure she would not have recommended settlement. I am also certain that she would have given the clients the opportunity to go to a jury trial if they wanted. At any rate, both the clients came in to meet with Ms. Cooperman and they must have agreed to settle because I was instructed several weeks later to have the clients sign the releases sent over by the defendant (which they did) and to prepare the disbursement papers for the clients.

The last time I heard from Mr. Engels and Ms. Rubin was when they came in to receive their checks. They both seemed quite upset with the amounts of their checks. I carefully went over with each of them the settlement papers to show that all the deductions from their award were consistent with the fee agreement they signed. (See Exhibit 6.) Both clients still appeared to be angry when they left and Mr. Engels said something about how he felt that Ms. Cooperman had cheated him. Rather than blasting him, I just bit my tongue and showed him the door. They just didn't appreciate that they were lucky to have Ms. Cooperman as their lawyer.

I had nothing else to do with these clients.

I have read this deposition and it is complete and accurate.

Pat Simpson

PAT SIMPSON

This deposition was taken in the office of the Respondent on January 18, YR-1. This deposition was given under oath, and was read and signed by the deponent.

Subscribed and sworn before me this 18th day of January, YR-0.

Harry Gibbons

HARRY GIBBONS
Certified Court Reporter

DEPOSITION OF HARRIET COOPERMAN[†]

My name is Harriet Cooperman. I am forty-two years old and live at 403 South Alder Street in Nita City. I am married to Robert Josephson, who is an advertising executive here in Nita City. We have two children, Rob, who is fourteen, and Joanne, who is twelve. I am a lawyer and the senior partner in the firm of Cooperman & Jones. I graduated from Nita University Law School in YR-17. I went to law school after receiving my undergraduate degree in Political Science from Nita U. in YR-20.

After graduating from law school I worked as an Assistant District Attorney for three years. In YR-14, I joined the law firm of Marks & Mayfield in Nita City, as an associate. In YR-10, another associate at Marks and Mayfield, Dan Jones, and I left the firm and formed our own firm, Cooperman & Jones. We have grown steadily over the years and now there are seven partners and thirteen associates in the firm. We also have ten paralegals as well as thirty-five secretarial and other support staff members. We are a general practice firm. I head up the litigation section. Dan Jones heads up our corporate and tax section. The litigation section has four partners, including myself, eight associates, and five paralegals. We do primarily plaintiff's personal injury work, including automobile negligence, products liability, and professional negligence cases, including against lawyers. The firm does a high volume of cases, and because we represent a lot of individuals on the litigation side and a number of corporations on the corporate and tax side of the firm, we had adopted a system to check on potential conflicts of interest before we accept a case—a system we have recently changed. The system that was in place at the time we represented Mr. Engels was primarily operated by our paralegals. Whenever a potential client came in for an initial interview, a litigation paralegal conducted an intake interview, obtaining the name and address of the potential client, the general nature of the potential cause of action, if known by the client (auto negligence, products liability, etc.), the date of the incident in question and the names and addresses of potential defendants. The paralegal then checked our computerized records to see if the firm currently represented any of the potential defendants. The client was then brought into one of the lawyers' offices. If no conflict existed, a full interview concerning the facts of the potential cause of action was conducted. If there was a conflict, the lawyer explained that the firm would be unable to represent the potential client unless the conflict was waived. I also explained the effect of the waiver to the parties, which in accident cases usually required one person to sue the other to insure a full recovery.

Since this matter arose, we reviewed and changed our recordkeeping policy to include the names, case names, and nature of the cases of past clients as well. This is something Jones and I had discussed a number of times after we realized how big we had become and the numerosity of our clients. We never got it done until these charges, albeit frivolous, gave some impetus to action. The firm began using the new conflict-checking system a few days ago, when the computer system's database was broadened. It is unusual, in my practice, that a conflict arises between a potential client and a former client of the firm, but we decided it was better to be safe than sorry.

One of our most typical situations initially handled by the paralegals is when two people involved in the same car accident come into the office for an interview together. Usually, one of the people drove

---

[†] The transcript of Harriet (Harry) Cooperman's deposition was excerpted so that only the answers are reprinted here. Assume that this is a true and accurate rendering of those answers.

one of the cars involved in the accident and the other was a passenger. The passenger hardly ever realizes that Nita law gives them a cause of action against the driver, who is usually a friend or a relative. Obviously, no matter who is at fault in the accident, the passenger is entitled to be fully compensated. The paralegal explains this to the potential clients and offers the passenger the opportunity to be interviewed separately by one of our lawyers. The potential clients are also given the opportunity to waive the conflict of interest inherent in the situation. If they want to be jointly represented, we include the waiver of the conflict in the fee agreement that our clients sign. (See EXHIBIT 4.)

David Engels and Mary Rubin are two former clients of mine who were in this situation. Ms. Rubin was driving the car and Mr. Engels was a passenger when they were involved in an accident with a truck that was owned by the Acme Paper Company. They were friends as well as colleagues on the faculty of the Lyman Hall High School in Nita City. Pat Simpson, one of our paralegals, conducted the initial interview of these two clients in September of YR-3. At that time Pat, who is a graduate of Nita University, had been working for us for about a year. Pat still works for us and now is also a second year evening division law student at Nita University School of Law. Pat is one of our best paralegals, whom I encouraged to attend law school. I anticipate Pat joining the firm as an associate after graduation and passing the bar.

As I said, Pat was the paralegal who worked on the Engels and Rubin case, conducting the initial interview of these people when they came to the office. While I wasn't there, I'm sure that Pat followed the procedure for discovering conflicts of interest that was in place at the time. I was the lawyer who conducted the in-depth interview of these clients in order to handle their case. I'm sure that Pat sat in on the interview as that was how we normally proceeded. While I don't have a specific recollection of the interview, I know that I obtained information about the injuries and losses suffered by both Engels and Rubin from reviewing my sketchy notes on the interview. (See EXHIBIT 5.)

I'm sure that I covered the particulars of the fee agreement with them, including the provision that the client pays all reasonable litigation costs, because that is my habit. In their case the fee agreement contained a written waiver of the potential conflict of interest between the two clients so I'm confident that I covered that portion of the agreement with them. Our procedure then in effect guaranteed, however, that Pat covered this with them, in detail as well, before I even met the clients.

Rubin and Engels were involved in a car accident while driving north on Broad Street in Nita City. As they approached the intersection of Montgomery Avenue, Ms. Rubin was distracted by a demonstration on that corner (which is near Nita University). By the time she returned her attention to the roadway, a southbound Acme Paper Truck turned left in front of her from Broad Street to Montgomery Avenue and a collision occurred. Rubin suffered a soft tissue injury to her back and had approximately $6,000 in medical bills plus $1,600 in lost earnings as a school teacher. (She took her pay in 9 increments during the school year.) Engels suffered a broken hip and arm and had approximately $28,000 in medicals plus $11,000 in lost earnings, also as a school teacher. They both had full medical insurance coverage and had no actual loss of income in that they had sufficient accumulated sick leave to cover their time off work.

I know that Rubin and Engels claim that I told them that they would receive $22,000 and $90,000 respectively for these claims during the initial meeting but I am sure that's not true. I never raise the expectations of clients in the initial interview by suggesting settlement amounts because you never know what will develop during the litigation. I'm sure that I told them that the case looked good, because it did, and that they could expect to be compensated for not only their medical bills and time off work, but for pain and suffering as well. I have looked at my notes from the first interview with Rubin and Engels in this case and I see that those numbers are on the page. I'm sure that the notes were just a rough calculation on my part of the likely place the cases would settle utilizing the multiplier of three which is common in Nita City.

The multiplier is a way of predicting how jurors will compensate a client for a particular injury. In Nita, if you multiply the medical bills times three and then add the loss of earnings, it gives you a rough guess as to a likely verdict by a jury. It is far from scientific and only applies in the most normal of cases. Any time you have facts or witnesses in a case who are better or worse than norm, the multiplier shifts appropriately. It can be as low as one and a half or as high as five. Of course, I had no way of knowing where, in that range, the Rubin and Engels cases would fall until the facts of the case were fully developed. I did tell them before negotiations on the lawsuit began that I was going to start the negotiations at approximately those figures ($22,000 and $90,000) and see where it led but that was in October of YR-I, some two years later. *[neog. plan]* *[this was estimate to start]*

The litigation against Acme Paper on behalf of Rubin and Engels was fairly routine. There were, however, two unusual things that did occur. First, even though I spent an hour each prepping Rubin and Engels for their depositions, they both came across horribly. Rubin was extremely hostile towards Jamie Doran, Acme's lawyer, and Engels acted as if Doran was holding a gun to his head the entire time; he was so nervous. Their respective demeanors during the deposition, *[depos.]* coupled with the fact that Rubin was distracted by the demonstrators on the corner, which she admitted during her deposition, led to the relatively low settlements on their cases. By way of contrast, Walt Brewer, the Acme Paper driver, was a real salt of the earth during his deposition.

Jamie Doran, who's nobody's fool, argued during negotiations that Rubin and Engels would both come across terribly with jurors, while Brewer would come across great, and based on their deposition performances, Doran was right. I told Jamie that with more preparation, the witness's demeanor problems could be overcome, but neither of us actually believed that (it is virtually impossible to change someone's personality). Jamie also pointed out that there was at least some negligence on the part of Rubin and, although I denied, Jamie might have gotten jurors to find Rubin 10–20 percent liable for the accident under Nita's comparative negligence statute. Of course, if Engels hadn't waived the conflict with Rubin and we'd represented him alone, I'm sure his case would have been worth more. *[believe reduce amt. would win @ trial]*

I started out the negotiation asking for $120,000 for Engels and $35,000 or so for Rubin hoping that we'd end up in the $70,000 and $22,000 range for settlement. Doran was particularly tough in these negotiations and would hear nothing of it. After all, Acme had a decent argument on both liability and the strength of the witnesses. Even so, I was able to get $16,000 for Rubin and $70,000 for Engels.

[- space during initial mtg.]

The other unusual thing that happened in this case is that Jamie Doran filed a motion to disqualify my firm from the case due to a conflict of interest. Acme Paper was not a current client at the time of the Rubin and Engels case. The former representation would not have been picked up in Pat's computer check. As of this January, our computer conflict check database includes former clients for a period of five years, but we weren't doing so in YR-3. I described the change earlier. I do not believe there was an actual conflict of interest in this situation but to be honest, it's better to avoid this kind of problem even if there is no professional responsibility violation, just to keep litigation costs to a minimum. As it developed in this case, one of our corporate partners, Gina Matthews, had represented Acme in YR-4 and early YR-3 in a reorganization that they underwent. That representation was over in March of YR-3. Doran claimed that because Acme was a self-insurer for accident claims, that the financial information that Gina received during the reorganization was related to the car/truck collision case because we could use that information in settlement negotiations. That motion was a loser for two reasons. First, I knew nothing about the Acme representation, much less the particulars of their financial condition, and second, the car/truck collision case had nothing to do whatsoever with the reorganization. I told Doran as much when we settled the Rubin and Engels cases. I am confident that this argument would never fly, and Doran admitted as much by settling before the motion was decided.

I don't like to mention this but I believe Doran has been out to get me ever since two years ago when I represented a client who had a legal professional negligence claim against Jamie. Doran had blown a statute of limitations in an open-and-shut contracts case for a former client. When Jamie tried to get out of it by telling the client that he had no case, the client came to me.

After investigating the case I presented the claim to Doran, whose malpractice insurance carrier settled for the full amount of the contract claim, which was only $35,000. I don't know why Jamie's so angry with me. I never told anybody (until now) about the claim. It was just a mistake and fortunately for the client, the client didn't have to pay for it. That's why we have malpractice insurance. Anyone can make a mistake. It was just Doran's turn. I certainly don't think any less of Jamie, who is a fine trial lawyer. If I didn't respect Jamie as a lawyer I wouldn't have settled the Rubin and Engels cases for the amount I did.

As I mentioned earlier, I met with Rubin and Engels in late September or early October of YR-1 to discuss potential settlement of the case. After a few minutes of conversation about the potential of going to trial and its potential benefits, both Rubin and Engels made it clear that they preferred settling the case, and avoiding the added expenses of trial and the need to testify. It was during this meeting that I told them that I was hoping to get offers of $85-95,000 for Engels and $20-25,000 for Rubin but that nothing was certain. I didn't raise the problems that Jamie Doran later pointed out (their demeanor at deposition and Rubin's negligence) because there was no need to upset the clients unless it was necessary.

The last contact I had with Rubin and Engels was in October of YR-1 after I had received what I believed to be Jamie Doran's last and best offer of settlement. I recommended to both Rubin and Engels that they settle the case for the offered amount because of the weaknesses in the case that I have mentioned earlier. They were both initially upset about the amounts. I first explained that Jamie Doran had taken the position that Rubin was comparatively negligent and that fact served to reduce the settlement offer. Engels in particular was upset because he couldn't understand why Rubin's comparative negligence should have anything to do with his settlement. I reminded him that against our standard advice in place then and now, he waived the conflict of interest with Rubin, and his right to sue her, at the outset of the lawsuit. I didn't like to do it, but I had to point out that together with the possible comparative negligence on the part of Rubin, the real reducing factor was that, based on their performance at deposition, Jamie Doran was convinced that they would not come across very well with jurors, and I had no argument to rebut this. They both also claimed that I had promised that their cases would settle for amounts in the $25,000 and $95,000 range. That's absurd and I told them so. I never promise any results because there is no certainty in this business. I told them that we could still go to trial but that I didn't recommend it. They never asked about the trial option and potential outcome. They finally agreed to settle the case and I communicated their agreement to Jamie Doran.

I know that Pat Simpson handled the signing of releases and the disbursement of money to Rubin and Engels and that they were upset with their final checks for the matter. All of the deductions from their portion of the settlement check were according to the fee agreement that they signed so I'm not sure what their complaint is. (See EXHIBIT 6.) The agreement was covered with them before they signed, so the deduction of costs of litigation from their portion of the settlement should not have come as a surprise.

I have given this deposition voluntarily although not required to do so. I have read this deposition and it is complete and accurate.

Harriet Cooperman
_____
HARRIET COOPERMAN

This deposition was taken in the office of the Respondent on January 12, YR-0. This deposition was given under oath, and was read and signed by the deponent.

Subscribed and sworn before me this 12th day of January, YR-0.

Harry Gibbons
_____
HARRY GIBBONS
Certified Court Reporter

DEPOSITION OF DAVID ENGELS[†]

My name is David Engels and I am thirty-one years old. I am married to my spouse, Jessie, who is a nurse, and we have one child, Terry, who is three years old. I work as a social studies teacher at Lyman Hall High School in Nita City. I have worked there since YR-9 when I received my undergraduate degree in education from Nita State University. I have since earned my Masters in Education from Nita University as a part time student. I received my Master's degree in YR-4.

In January of YR-4 I was involved in a car accident near the Nita University campus. I was a passenger in Mary Rubin's car (Mary was also a teacher at the school) when we ran into an Acme Paper Company truck that turned left in front of us. At the time of the accident we were traveling north on Broad Street on our way to an evening Graduate School of Education class that both Mary and I were enrolled in. I had just pointed out to Mary a bunch of kids demonstrating about the environment on the corner of Broad and Montgomery when the Acme Paper Company truck just turned left in front of us. Mary tried to stop but couldn't and we got into a terrible wreck. I broke both my hip and my right arm. Mary hurt her back. I ended up missing two months of school before I was able to get around sufficiently to teach my classes. I also had extensive medical bills. Fortunately, I had accumulated enough sick leave that I didn't lose any pay; otherwise, I would have lost close to $11,000 in income. All of my medical bills, which totaled approximately $28,000, were covered between my health insurance and my wife's health insurance.

I was very lucky and completely recovered from my injuries. Because I wasn't out any money, and because I don't much care for lawyers (they always seem to be so officious), I had no real intention to sue anybody over the accident. The driver of the truck was very nice to me at the time of the accident and even helped to get me out of the car so I could be loaded into the ambulance. I didn't see any reason to cause him a lot of grief. I think Mary felt the same way until she got her new car insurance rates from her insurance company. Mary had gotten her car repaired under her collision coverage, and because she wasn't out of pocket anything other than her $250 deductible on her collision coverage, she didn't think it was worth going to a lawyer. When she got her new insurance bill and her rates almost doubled because of the accident, she changed her mind in a hurry.

Mary told me that she had been referred by one of her neighbors to a lawyer named Harriet Cooperman, who apparently had represented the neighbor in a car accident case. Because Mary was going to the lawyer I agreed to go along, just to see what would happen.

When we arrived at the law firm, we were introduced to a young paralegal named Pat Simpson. Pat wanted some preliminary information from us before we met with Ms. Cooperman. We told Pat that we were involved in a car accident and the date of the accident, that Mary was driving and I was a passenger, and that the truck involved in the accident was owned by the Acme Paper Company and driven by a man named Walter Brewer. At that point Pat informed us that

---

[†] The transcript of David Engels' deposition was excerpted so that only the answers are reprinted here. Assume that this is a true and accurate rendering of those answers.

I had a case against Mary if I wanted to sue her and that if I did, the firm could only represent one of us and not the other. Because I thought the accident was the truck driver's fault, I was a little taken aback by that comment. Pat asked me to think about it and went to check something in the computer.

Mary and I talked for a minute and I decided that we wouldn't even be at the office if it hadn't been for Mary's insurance and the last thing she needed was someone suing her. When Pat returned I said that I felt that the accident was the fault of the truck driver and that I really didn't want to sue my friend. Pat said that was fine and that we could then both go in to see Ms. Cooperman.

Ms. Cooperman was very businesslike with us. She asked if Pat had explained that I could sue Mary if I wanted, and I said that I had decided not to sue her. She did not tell me that if I sued Mary it would be in name only; that any payments would come from Mary's insurance company. I can't say for sure what my response would have been, because Mary's insurance rates were the reason we were there and I assumed if I sued her insurance company her rates would be even more. At any rate I received no explanation or counseling on this from Cooperman.

That was the total of our conversation about that issue. Cooperman then asked all about the accident and we told her everything. She didn't seem concerned about the fact that we had been distracted by the demonstrators. At least she didn't say so. We informed her about our medical bills and how long we were out of work. Apparently, according to Ms. Cooperman, even though we didn't actually lose any income because of sick leave, nor had to pay any medical bills because of insurance, we were entitled to receive those amounts from the Acme Paper Company. She also said that we were entitled to receive money for our pain and suffering. I expressed some concern about suing Mr. Brewer, who had been so nice to me after the accident. She also assured us that it would be Acme or their insurance company that paid for the accident, not the driver Mr. Brewer. No, that did not make me understand that Mary's insurance company would be paying damages if I sued her.

I specifically remember Mary asking Ms. Cooperman how the case looked and Cooperman said that when someone turns left in front of you, it is usually that person's fault. When Mary asked how much money we could get if everything went "OK" Cooperman said that she couldn't be certain, but that we were looking in the neighborhood of $90–100,000 for me and $20–25,000 for Mary. She did say that this was just a rough guess and that anything could happen in the litigation and that we hadn't heard the truck driver's side of the story but she didn't change her estimate of the value of the case. To say the least, I was shocked. I only make $65,000 in a year so $90,000 seemed like an enormous amount of money to me.

Cooperman also told us that we wouldn't have to pay her unless we received money for the case; that if we received money that her fee would be one-third of whatever we received. She then asked if we wanted her to undertake our representation. We both agreed and she had us sign a fee agreement. (See EXHIBIT 4.) I know now that the fee agreement provided that I gave up the right to sue Mary and that we were responsible for the "costs" of the litigation, but to be honest, I was so surprised by the $90,000 figure that I wasn't focusing on what I was signing.

Ms. Cooperman may have said something about the so-called "costs" being our responsibility, I can't swear she didn't, but it couldn't have been very clear because to this day I don't remember being told about the "cost," and what the costs of litigation were and about how much they would be.

Costs of Litigation (handwritten margin note)

I guess the case proceeded the way they normally do. I have no way to tell really. I know that it seemed forever before anything happened in the case. I had very little contact with Ms. Cooperman. Whenever I called her with a question she never got on the phone. Sometimes Pat Simpson would call me right back. Sometimes I would have to call several times before Pat would call and answer my questions. They did tell me that it would take several years for the case to come to trial but it seemed like once we signed up with them that they really didn't want to have anything to do with either of us.

The only time I had any contact with Ms. Cooperman before the case eventually settled was in January of YR-1 when my deposition was taken. I don't mind telling you that I was more than a little intimidated by the prospect of being grilled by some lawyer and Ms. Cooperman didn't do anything to help me over that. In fact, when we talked about the deposition on the morning before it happened, she made a point of telling me how the other lawyer was out to get me and to be sure to listen carefully to his questions so that I wasn't fooled. She practically yelled at me when we were practicing before the deposition, not to answer anything but the most narrow response to the other lawyer's questions. To make matters worse, they were predicting a snowstorm and I was worried about getting my son from daycare in time because my wife was working overtime that week in the Emergency Room at Memorial Hospital.

By the time the deposition started I was a nervous wreck. As it turned out the other lawyer, Jamie Doran, was actually rather nice to me. Just when I was getting comfortable, Ms. Cooperman took a break and took me outside and berated me for volunteering too much information—for answering more than the question asked for. That put me back on edge. In addition, Cooperman started interrupting both me and the other lawyer during the deposition. I guess she was just doing her job, but it was sure nerve wracking. It didn't seem to affect her or Doran, who virtually ignored her interruptions, and afterwards she seemed pleased with how the deposition went.

I didn't hear from her again until late September or early October of YR-1. At that time Mary and I went into her office and we talked about the case. Cooperman told us that she was going to meet with the lawyer for Acme and try to settle the case and she wanted to discuss the case with us first. She told us that she was going to try to settle the case for $95,000 for me and $25,000 for Mary based on our respective medical bills and time out of work. I remember asking her if we got interest from the time of bringing the lawsuit and she told us, unfortunately not. The reason I asked, even though I didn't tell her specifically, was because the amounts of money she mentioned were about the same that she gave us two years before. When we told her that the amounts sounded good to us, she told us that she'd meet with Acme's lawyer and get back to us in the near future.

She never talked to us about going to trial. It was as if that wasn't an option. To be honest, given my experience at the deposition, I was relieved. Don't get me wrong. I was willing to go to trial, especially if it meant the difference of a lot of money. I just wasn't looking forward to it.

About a week later, we got a call from Pat Simpson asking us to come in to see Ms. Cooperman for the purpose of discussing an offer to settle. We met with her on October 10, YR-1. After some small talk she told us that Acme's last and best offer was $70,000 for me and $16,000 for Mary. Both Mary and I were surprised, and I remember asking Cooperman if that was before her fee or after. She said before, that her one-third fee would be deducted from that amount. She did not mention deducting costs. I asked her what had happened to the $90–95,000 she had talked about. She was very condescending and explained that the settlement was less for two reasons.

First, she said that the accident was at least partially Mary's fault and that Acme's lawyer had made a good argument for reducing the amount due to us by 20 percent because the accident was at least 20 percent Mary's fault. When I complained that the accident certainly wasn't my fault, Cooperman got nasty and said that I shouldn't have waived my right to sue Mary if I wanted a full recovery. When we both asked how the accident could be 20 percent Mary's fault when the truck turned in front of us and we couldn't avoid it, Cooperman gave her second reason. She said that Mary had been hostile in the deposition and that I was acting real nervous and that jurors picked up on those things and for that reason alone our cases were worth less than she originally thought. When I asked Cooperman why she hadn't raised this problem before, she said that she was hoping that Jamie Doran wouldn't pick up on our bad demeanor but, unfortunately, had.

We then raised the issue of going to trial. Ms. Cooperman was very negative on this idea. She said that, based on almost twenty years of experience, we should take the settlement and be happy with it, but it was our decision and if we wanted a trial we could have one. Because I didn't think I could argue with her, I agreed with the settlement. I know from talking to Mary that she felt the same way.

About a week later we again got a call from Pat Simpson and went to the law office and signed releases. A week after that we returned. Ms. Cooperman did not meet with us. Pat Simpson had our checks and an accounting statement detailing the way final amounts were determined. (See Exhibit 6.) I was surprised at the amount of costs that were deducted from my portion of the settlement. There were deductions for expert witness fees and court reporter fees and Xeroxing fees and telephone calls and cabs. I even had to pay for lunch for myself and Cooperman on the day of the deposition. When I asked about these costs, Pat got real defensive and pulled out our fee agreement (Exhibit 4) and pointed out that I had agreed to pay all necessary expenses of the litigation. As I said earlier, I signed the agreement but I really didn't understand fully what it meant. Because I didn't think there was anything I could do about it, I signed the accounting and took my check.

I'll have to admit that the whole process left a sour taste in my mouth. Several weeks later I was at my son's daycare center for a kids' Halloween party. One of the other parents at the party was Jamie Doran, who had been the lawyer for the Acme Paper Company. We got to talking and it came up that I felt that Ms. Cooperman hadn't done a very good job on my case. Doran told me that if I had any problems with the representation that I should report Cooperman to the Bar Association. When I tried to get into the details of how I thought I had been mistreated by

Cooperman, Doran told me that if I complained to the Bar Association that they would probably call Doran as a witness, so it was inappropriate to get into the specifics with me. When I asked if that meant that Doran agreed that Cooperman hadn't done a good job, I couldn't get a straight answer, but Doran repeated that if I had problems with the representation that I should report Cooperman to the Bar Association. I <u>took this as agreement that she had done a bad job.</u>

Because I was still angry with the way I had been treated by Cooperman, and because her conduct wasn't how I think a lawyer should be, I decided to report her to the Bar Association. I talked it over with Mary Rubin, but she told me that she was moving with her family to Pennsylvania, in January of YR-0, to take a job as an Assistant Superintendent of Schools, and although she agreed with me that she didn't want to get involved.

I have read this deposition and it is complete and accurate.

DAVID ENGELS

This deposition was taken in the office of the State Bar of Nita on January 20, YR-0. This deposition was given under oath and was read and signed by the deponent.

Subscribed and sworn before me this 20th day of January, YR-0.

Harry Gibbons

HENRY GIBBONS
Certified Court Reporter

DEPOSITION OF JAMIE DORAN[§]

My name is Jamie Doran and I am thirty-seven years old. I am married to Hayden Richards, who is also a lawyer. We are both partners in the firm of Bains and Montgomery here in Nita City.

We have two children, Casey, who is four years old, and Tatum, who is two. My practice is as a litigator. I represent a number of insurance carriers as well as a number of corporations that self-insure for personal injury liability. My work is exclusively as a personal injury defense lawyer. I am giving this deposition at the request of the Nita Bar Association.

One of my clients is the Acme Paper Company. Our firm represents Acme for their full range of legal services and has done so since September of YR-4. One of my first cases for Acme involved a car/truck accident that took place in January of YR-4. The plaintiffs in the case were Mary Rubin and David Engels. They were involved in an accident with one of Acme's trucks that took place when the truck, which was traveling south on Broad Street, made a left onto Montgomery Avenue and was struck by the plaintiffs' car that was northbound on Broad Street. The accident was the fault of our driver, who failed to yield the right of way to the plaintiffs. Ms. Rubin, who was the driver of the plaintiffs' car, admitted to being distracted directly before the collision took place by some demonstrators on the corner of Broad and Montgomery, but that was of little or no causal effect to the accident.

Ms. Rubin suffered a soft tissue injury to her back for which she sustained approximately $6,000 worth of medical treatment and missed work for a week to her loss of $1,600. Mr. Engels was more seriously injured, suffering a broken arm and hip, and had approximately $28,000 in medical treatments and was out of work for two months for an earnings loss of approximately $11,000. Because the liability was clear, this was really a damages case for me. I was initially hoping to get out of the case for $80–105,000 for Engels and $18–25,000 for Rubin.

The lawyer on the other side was Harriet Cooperman of Cooperman and Jones. She is a well-known plaintiff's personal injury lawyer in Nita City. I had several cases with her firm before this one, but never with her. She has a reputation as a hard-nosed litigator who gets decent results for her clients. Her entire firm, at least on the litigation side, has a similar reputation. Litigation against C & J is always very contentious. It's not the way I like to practice law, but it seems to get good results for their clients so I can't really fault them.

I had one personal experience with Harriet Cooperman before the Acme case. She represented one of my former clients in a legal malpractice claim against me. The claim was that I failed to file a cause of action in a timely way for a client and that as a result the client missed the statute of limitations on a small contracts case that the client claimed was worth $35,000. Cooperman called me and threatened the filing of a lawsuit unless the case could be settled. I notified my malpractice carrier. It was my recollection that I told the client that I wasn't interested in taking the contract claim because it was outside my area of expertise and suggested

---

[§] The transcript of James Doran's deposition was excerpted so that only the answers are reprinted here. Assume that this is a true and accurate rendering of those answers.

that he seek other counsel. The client insisted that although I told him I wouldn't take the case that he believed that another lawyer in my firm was going to represent him. When he called to inquire about this supposed representation by my firm, I told him that we were not representing him. In the interim, the statute of limitations had passed. Even though I didn't believe that we had done anything wrong, it was my word against the client's, and because it would cost almost as much to litigate the case as to settle it, we settled the case before suit was instituted for $35,000.

I don't hold any grudges against Cooperman because of that situation. After all she was just doing her job. I'll have to admit that at the time, I was a little perturbed at her, more for her holier-than-thou attitude towards me than the fact of the lawsuit. No matter, that doesn't have anything to do with my testimony here. As I said, I didn't complain to the Bar Association in this matter. I'm testifying because they asked me to cooperate, so I am.

Back to the Acme case; we did get two breaks in the case.

The first was that both Ms. Rubin and Mr. Engels didn't come across very well in their depositions. Ms. Rubin was very hostile and aggressive and I thought this wouldn't sell well with jurors given that her injuries, soft tissue sprain and strain to the back, are so "iffy" to begin with. Mr. Engels was extremely nervous and came across as if he had something to hide even though, in reality, I believe that he was completely forthcoming. After all, he was the passenger. The accident certainly couldn't be his fault and his injuries were both real and substantial.

Frankly, I was a little surprised that both Rubin and Engels were represented by the same lawyer. I guess they figured that Rubin's liability was so minimal that any suit against her by Engels (who was a friend) was more trouble than it was worth. As to Engels's lack of comfort as a witness, I believe that he was unnerved by Cooperman's tactics of constantly interrupting the deposition by making needless comments and objections.

The second break was that, in my opinion, Cooperman had a conflict of interest. This had no effect on the liability but could force the plaintiffs to get a new lawyer which would delay the case and allow us to keep our money a little longer. In late YR-4 and early YR-3 one of Cooperman's partners, Gina Matthews, represented Acme Paper Company in a corporate reorganization. As a result, C & J was privy to confidential information as to the financial condition of Acme Paper Company. Because Acme is a self-insurer, I felt the previous representation by C & J was substantially related to their representation against Acme in the Rubin and Engels case. They were in possession of confidential financial information as well as information about Acme's assets that could be used against Acme in settlement negotiations. When you know the financial condition of your opponent so intimately, it is possible to make sophisticated judgments as to how much a client might be willing to pay in a given case. As a result of the above, I filed a motion to disqualify Cooperman and her firm from the case against Acme.

substantially related

It is correct that the financial information of Acme did not come into play in this case, but that is not the test as I understand it. I made the motion because I believed the conflict was real, even though not actually operative in this case. It certainly could have been.

As it turned out, the motion was never decided by the court because we settled the case. I obviously discussed the motion with Cooperman both before and after filing it. She took the position, an incorrect one in my view, that because she had no actual knowledge of the financial condition of Acme, there was no conflict. She also argued that even if the information was imputed to her, it didn't create a conflict because the two representations by her firm were not related. Even though I disagreed with her, I agreed to discuss settling the case at her suggestion. After all, her clients had a legitimate claim and if it could be settled reasonably, there was no reason not to.

During the negotiations with Cooperman I argued, albeit halfheartedly, that the accident was at least 20 percent the fault of Rubin because of her being distracted by the demonstrators. I also pointed out that her clients, based on their performance in the depositions, would not make good witnesses and that was another reason to devalue the case. Cooperman started out demanding $120,000 for Engels and $35,000 for Rubin. I started out at $60,000 and $12,000 respectively. After about an hour Cooperman had to concede the weakness of her witnesses and, surprisingly, the possibility that Rubin would be found partially liable. She demanded $95,000 and $22,000. These amounts were almost exactly on the multiplier system that is used to roughly calculate settlement values in Nita City. The theory is that if you multiply the medical expenses of the plaintiff times three and then add the loss of earnings, that you can come to a reasonable guess as to what jurors would return in a given case. The multiplier varies from one-and-a-half to about five, based on the strength and attractiveness of the case.

The three multiplier was, in my opinion, fair in this case, but I argued with her some more, merely covering the same ground, and offered $70,000 and $16,000. I expected her to reject this offer, but to my surprise she agreed to recommend the settlement to her clients. Quite frankly, I expected her to come back and tell me that her clients wouldn't accept the offer and make a higher demand, but several days later she called to accept the offer. I sent her a release for her clients and after receiving the signed release, checks were immediately sent.

I'll admit that after the case settled, I thought back on the negotiation, and came to the opinion that the reason Cooperman was so compliant was not because of my arguments, but because she was concerned about losing the conflict of interest motion and her fee. Of course, I can't be sure that's the case. I never argued or implied that she should settle the case to avoid being conflicted out, but on reflection I think that's more than a possibility. Yes, you're right, that is just my opinion, but it is more than speculation.

Several week later I ran into one of the plaintiffs in the Acme case, David Engels. Apparently his son goes to the same daycare center as my younger child, and we met at a Halloween party there. We recognized each other from the deposition, but to be honest, I didn't remember who he was until he introduced himself. We were making some small talk when he brought up the fact that he was unhappy with the way he had been treated by his lawyer. I really didn't want to get involved, so I told him the same thing I say when anyone complains to me about their lawyer; that they have the option to complain to the Bar Association if they are unhappy. This is usually enough to change the subject and my experience is that few, if any, people actually make a formal complaint. Mr. Engels was more persistent, however, and tried to get into the particulars of his complaint. I told him that I really couldn't get into it with him; that he should call Cooperman if he was unhappy. When he persisted, I told him that if he did complain to the Bar Association that I would probably be a witness, so it would be improper for me to speak with him about his complaints. I really didn't think that I would be a witness. I just said that to get him off my back. I certainly didn't mean to suggest that I thought he had a legitimate complaint because I don't know enough about the whole representation by Cooperman to come to an opinion. I have provided testimony today knowing the nature of the complaint by Engels and have provided answers to your questions.

I have read this deposition and it is complete and accurate.

Jamie Doran

JAMIE DORAN

This deposition was taken in the office of the State Bar of Nita on January 20, YR-0. This deposition was given under oath, and was read and signed by the deponent.

Subscribed and sworn before me this 20th day of January, YR-0.

Harry Gibbons

HARRY GIBBONS
Certified Reporter

EXPERT DEPOSITIONS

DEPOSITION OF COSME GALLO**

My name is Cosme Gallo. I live at 100 E. Falls Drive in Nita City with my spouse, Kendall, and two children Charlie and Frankie. I am forty-two years old and practice law with the firm of Roberts, Gallo & Wallach. My qualifications are listed in my resume, which was provided with my Rule 26[††] expert report. I believe it has been has been marked separately as EXHIBIT 1. I have been hired by the lawyers for Harriet Cooperman to serve as an expert witness in the matter now before the Nita Disciplinary Board. It is also understood that I will serve as an expert witness should there arise any civil litigation against Ms. Cooperman based on the same facts underlying this disciplinary proceeding.

I have served as an expert witness in legal professional negligence cases on eight occasions in the past four years, twice for plaintiffs and six times for defendants. In both cases for plaintiffs I was retained by Ms. Cooperman's firm to serve as an expert witness. Three of the cases in which I was retained went to trial. In all the cases in which I testified, the jurors returned a verdict for the party for whom I testified (including the two for the Cooperman firm). I have never served as an expert witness in a disciplinary hearing.

I am compensated for the time I spend as an expert witness at the rate of $500 per hour. To date I have spent eleven hours on this matter, and have received payment for my time in the amount of $5,500. I will be compensated for my time at this deposition and any time required for trial preparation and testimony at the same rate of $600 per hour.

I have never been a witness for or against Ms. Cooperman as a party in the past. I have known her for ten years, however, and consider her to be a professional friend; that is, we socialize at bar meetings and the like, but not otherwise. I know Harriet Cooperman to be a talented, hard-nosed plaintiff's lawyer, whose character for honesty is beyond reproach. In addition, her firm has referred several clients with white collar criminal problems to our office. We have reciprocated by referring legal professional negligence claims to her office. This arrangement has worked out well because the Cooperman firm does not do any criminal work, and our firm does not handle legal professional negligence claims. We did not refer this case to the Cooperman firm.

I have reviewed all of the pleadings in this matter, the depositions of the parties and fact witnesses, the exhibits, and the applicable Model Rules of Professional Conduct. In addition, I spoke to Ms. Gina Matthews, Ms. Cooperman's law partner. I have also reviewed the deposition of Professor Basara, the expert witness for the Nita State Bar. I do not know Professor Basara, except by reputation as a well-known plaintiff's professional negligence witness. We never met during the brief time Basara practiced as a corporate lawyer here in Nita City. That is not surprising given that my practice is almost exclusively in plaintiff's personal injury and white collar criminal litigation.

** The transcript of Gallo's deposition is excerpted so that only the answers are reprinted. Assume the parties agree that this is a true and accurate and complete rendering of those answers.

[††] Assume that the Nita Rules of Civil Procedure apply in Disciplinary Board proceedings and are identical to the FRCP.

I should say at the outset that this case would never have come to the charging stage while I was an associate counsel for the Nita State Bar in the Office of Disciplinary Counsel. The alleged violations are hyper-technical in nature and seem to be the result of a disgruntled client, unhappy with the outcome of his lawsuit. In my opinion this case does not belong before the Disciplinary Board. This case should be litigated, if at all, in the civil courts where the parties are governed by Rule 11,[‡‡] and can be made to answer for inappropriate pleading.

For the purposes of this opinion, I have assumed the following facts to be true. Ms. Cooperman represented David Engels, the complaining witness here, in a routine car accident case during the period of September YR-3 through October YR-1. Engels was a passenger in a car driven by a Ms. Rubin, which collided with an Acme Paper Company truck. At the time of the collision, the truck had made a left turn in front of the Rubin vehicle. At approximately the same time, Rubin was distracted from her lane of traffic by some demonstrators on the side of the street.

Engels and Rubin came to Ms. Cooperman seeking representation. They were interviewed by Pat Simpson, a paralegal in Ms. Cooperman's office, and informed by Simpson that, if Engels desired, he could sue Rubin, along with the Acme Paper Company, for the injuries he received. Engels was also offered an interview with Ms. Cooperman outside the presence of Rubin. He declined both to sue Rubin and to be interviewed privately.

Engels and Rubin were then interviewed by Ms. Cooperman. She also explained the potential of a cause of action by Engels against Rubin a second time. Engels, once again, declined to sue his friend.

Engels decided to retain Ms. Cooperman, and signed a standard contingent fee agreement. The agreement, which was fully explained by Ms. Cooperman to Engels, contains a waiver of the conflict of interest between Engels and Rubin. (EXHIBIT 4.)

The lawsuit on behalf of Engels and Rubin against the Acme Paper Company was filed by Ms. Cooperman and proceeded in a rather routine way. During the depositions of Engels and Rubin, however, both testified in a manner that caused Jamie Doran, the counsel for Acme, to believe that they would not be effective witnesses. Ms. Cooperman privately recognized the validity of Doran's evaluation (though she never admitted to Doran that she agreed with that evaluation).

As the trial date for the lawsuit neared, Doran filed a motion to disqualify Cooperman from representing her clients based on a supposed conflict of interest. The motion claimed that because Ms. Cooperman's partner had represented the Acme Paper Company in a reorganization in late YR-4 and early YR-3 Ms. Cooperman should be deemed to have a vicarious conflict of interest that precluded her from suing the Acme Paper Company. Ms. Cooperman considered this motion frivolous, as do I.

Ms. Cooperman met with her clients in September of YR-1 and discussed the possibility of settlement. Both clients were amenable to settlement, and actually preferred settlement to trial.

[‡‡] See FRCP 11.

Ms. Cooperman then entered into negotiations with Jamie Doran, who argued forcefully that neither Engels nor Rubin were particularly persuasive witnesses and, despite all attempts by Ms. Cooperman at raising the settlement offer, a final offer was made for both Engels ($70,000) and Rubin ($16,000). Doran, who was previously successfully sued by Ms. Cooperman in a professional negligence matter, now claims a willingness and expectation to have to go higher—that is unreliable.

Ms. Cooperman then met with her clients to discuss the offers. After consultation, and considering the trial option, the clients decided to accept the settlement offers. The cases were settled and the clients received the proceeds of the settlement after appropriate deduction of fees and costs. Both clients signed Disbursal of Settlement forms in October of YR-1.

After a conversation with Jamie Doran in October of YR-1, Engels brought the instant complaint against Ms. Cooperman to the Nita State Bar.

I am of the opinion that Harriet Cooperman did not violate the Model Rules of Professional Conduct in her representation of Engels and Rubin in their lawsuit against the Acme Paper Company. I will be happy to consider each claim and state the reason for my opinion with regard to each of them.

The State Bar claims that Ms. Cooperman violated Rule 1.5(c) with regard to the setting of fees. This is the most hyper-technical of all of the charges. Rule 1.5(c) provides that "A contingent fee shall be in writing signed by the client and state the method by which the fee is to be determined, . . . and other expenses to be deducted from the recovery, and whether such expenses are to be deducted before or after the contingent fee is deducted."

According to Professor Basara, Ms. Cooperman violated this rule because her fee agreement was not written in the exact words of the rule. There is no such requirement stated in Rule 1.5(c). The Cooperman/Engels fee agreement is clear. It provides that the fee is "equal to thirty-three and one-third percent (33 1/3%) of the total amount of any recovery," and that the client is responsible "for all reasonable and necessary expenses incurred." The agreement is unambiguous as to the fact that "all" expenses are to be paid by the client and that the fee is one-third of the "total" amount of any recovery. There is no way to read this agreement to say that one-third of the expenses are to be paid by the lawyer, which is the net effect of deducting the expenses from the total amount of the award and then calculating the one-third contingent fee. (See EXHIBIT 4.)

The State Bar also claims that there was a conflict of interest between Ms. Cooperman and her clients. This claim of conflict is premised on another alleged conflict of interest between Ms. Cooperman and the Acme Paper Company, the former client of one of her partners. These claims are intertwined in that the State Bar alleges that when the Acme Paper Company filed its motion to disqualify Ms. Cooperman premised on an imputed conflict of interest between her and the Acme Paper Company, this motion caused her to settle Engels's case for a lower than appropriate amount to save her fee. It is appropriate, then, to consider first, the viability of the claim of imputed conflict of interest.

Rule I.10 provides that no lawyer (here Cooperman) can knowingly represent a client when one of her partners would be prohibited from doing so by, among other rules, Rule 1.9. Rule 1.9 provides that a lawyer may not represent a current client (here, Engels and Rubin) in a cause of action against a former client (here Acme Paper Company) where the subject matter of the cause of action is "substantially related" to the representation of the former client. The purpose of this rule is to prevent attorneys from using confidential information gained in the course of a representation to the later detriment of a client. The conflict of interest is imputed because there is a presumption that partners share information.

In late YR-4 and early YR-3, Ms. Cooperman's partner, Gina Matthews, represented Acme in a corporate reorganization. During that time, Ms. Matthews was apparently privy to confidential financial information. Because Acme is a self-insurer, the State Bar now claims that the corporate reorganization of Acme in YR-4 and YR-3 is somehow substantially related to the potential settlement of a car/truck accident in YR-1. This charge is invalid for a number of reasons.

First, even though there is a presumption of shared information among partners, there is no credible evidence that there was actual sharing of Acme's confidences between Ms. Matthews and Ms. Cooperman. Both Ms. Cooperman and Ms. Matthews deny there ever was any exchange of information. If the purpose of the rule is to prevent use of such confidences against a former client, that purpose has not been violated here.

The Cooperman & Jones law firm has two distinct and separate sections. On the day to day handling of the business of each section, there is little or no communication of information regarding confidences of the respective clients of the lawyers in each section. In fact, there was no such communication here. The Disciplinary Board should not apply the rules in such a way as to ignore the reality of modern day law practice, where the fact of partnership does not in any way guarantee sharing client confidences. I was most surprised by the Professor's contrary opinion on this issue, because his YR-4 article in the University of Nita Law Review makes my very point and argues that imputation among partners in different sections of law firms, absent a showing of a particular sharing of a particular confidence, or the regularity of sharing client confidences among sections as a firm practice, is inappropriate.

Second, even if the rules are applied mechanically, there is no violation here. The key phrase in Rule 1.9 is "substantially related." As stated earlier, there is no substantial relationship between a corporate reorganization in YR-4 and a car/truck accident settlement in YR-1. Certainly the facts are not the same, nor are the witnesses. There is no evidence that the truck driver involved in this wreck was one of the players in the corporate reorganization of YR-4. Professor Basara's deposition suggests that because Acme is a self-insurer that the financial information of YR-4 is helpful in formulating settlement strategy in the Engels/Rubin lawsuit. Not only is this claim insupportable on the facts in the case, it is preposterous on its face. The information received by Matthews was two to three years old when the settlement discussions occurred and therefore stale. If it ever had any utility in settlement discussions, that utility was gone by YR-1. In addition, the ability of Acme to pay a settlement is easily discoverable during the litigation process, and there is nothing to suggest, including consultation by Doran, whether the company had any finance-related limitations on Doran's settlement authority, a fact admitted in Doran's deposition.

Given the weakness of the imputed conflict of interest claim, the alleged conflict of interest between Ms. Cooperman and her clients that supposedly followed from Mr. Doran's motion to disqualify on imputed disqualification grounds, is equally unprovable. Professor Basara suggests that Ms. Cooperman had a conflict between herself and her clients because she settled their lawsuits for lower than appropriate amounts in order to save her fee. This claim also lacks any merit for the following reasons.

First, Ms. Cooperman viewed the Doran motion as frivolous, and no one, not even Doran, who has built-in prejudice against Ms. Cooperman, suggests that she ever said anything that would suggest the contrary. If she did not feel the motion was meritorious, it certainly could not affect her judgment to the level necessary to create a conflict of interest. In addition, Doran knew that the claim was meritless—Acme never provided any information that their financial condition mandated certain negotiation limitations that applied to the Engels case. Second, Doran did not seek a ruling on the disqualification motion before entering into settlement negotiations, and certainly did not heavily rely on the motion in any negotiation tactics as described by either attorney.

Second, the facts are clear that the reasons for the settlement figures that were reached in the case were the potential liability of Rubin for the accident, given her lack of attention to the roadway, and the credibility and persuasiveness of Engels and Rubin as trial witnesses, based on their performances at the deposition. These were the points argued by Doran during the settlement negotiations, and they are certainly legitimate bases for the settlement offer that was made. How the witness appears and their demeanor as witnesses, as every trial lawyer knows, has a great deal to do with the amount of damages jurors will award. It is true that some demeanor issues can be addressed in preparation for trial, but these issues were mainly a product of the personalities of the witnesses demonstrated throughout the litigation, which cannot be changed by preparation.

Finally, on this issue, even if Ms. Cooperman was disqualified from representing Engels and Rubin, she would not have lost her fee completely. The case would have been referred to another lawyer who could then settle or try the case, and Ms. Cooperman would still be entitled to the fair value of the fee earned based on the amount of work she had performed. Because the motion was not filed until the eleventh hour, virtually all the work in the case had been completed. All that remained was either a settlement or a rather straightforward trial. To suggest that a lawyer of the quality and character of Ms. Cooperman would settle a lawsuit to the detriment of a client to protect some small portion of a fee is a failure to recognize the real world of law practice in a competitive market where reputation and recommendations of former clients is of paramount importance.

The State Bar also alleges that Ms. Cooperman violated Rule 1.7 by simultaneously representing two clients with conflicting interests. In the terms of this case, the claim is that because Engels had a potential cause of action against Rubin that it was inappropriate for Ms. Cooperman to represent the two of them.

While it is true that there was a conflict of interest between Engels and Rubin, the rules provide that the conflict can be waived by the clients after consultation. Professor Basara contends that this conflict was of the sort that could not be waived. I disagree. These clients were friends. They were also highly educated individuals. The conflict of interest was explained to them twice, once by Pat Simpson and once by Ms. Cooperman. On both occasions it was waived, primarily because of the relationship between the clients. In addition, the fee agreement between Cooperman and Engels also contained the waiver. (See Exhibit 4.) Engels's claim of not understanding the effect of the waiver, after three opportunities to choose to have separate counsel, is just not credible, given his level of education.

It was certainly Cooperman's duty to explain the conflict and the effect of doing so. She met this burden, both orally and in writing, as well as through the vehicle of her paralegal, Pat Simpson.

Finally, the State Bar makes a broad claim that Ms. Cooperman failed to adequately consult with her clients. Professor Basara states that the failure to consult occurred in the context of first, not explaining to the clients the full range of options to settlement of the lawsuit (i.e. the trial option) and second, in failing to inform the clients of the pending motion to disqualify Cooperman, as it might affect settlement value of the case. The facts of the case simply do not support these claims.

Ms. Cooperman discussed the trial option with her clients and even Engels agrees that he preferred to settle the case rather than go to trial. He had both options and chose to settle. There was no need to raise the disqualification motion with the clients because, in the mind of Ms. Cooperman, as well as in my opinion, consistent with the evidence, and the testimony of Doran, the motion had no merit. Because the motion had no effect on the litigation of the case, (there was not even a scheduled date for consideration by the trial court), there was no need to speak to the clients about it. If, in fact, the motion did have merit in the opinion of Ms. Cooperman, then the possibility of a conflict would have existed, and she would have been required to raise the issue with her clients.

In response to your question, I recognize the treatise, THE NITA LAW OF PROFESSIONAL RESPONSIBILITY, by Professor John Wellman as an authoritative text on the law of professional responsibility in Nita and have relied on it in the rendering of my opinions in this matter. I also read a law review article by the Board's expert.

I have read this deposition and it is complete and accurate.

Cosme Gallo

The deposition was taken pursuant to an agreement between counsel to depose the expert witnesses in the case. It was taken in the offices of the counsel for the Nita State Bar. The deposition was given under oath, and was read and signed by the deponent.

Subscribed and sworn before me this 30th day of January, YR-0.

Harry Gibbons

_____

Harry Gibbons
Certified Court Reporter

Exhibit 1

2039 Aspen Way
Nita Park, Nita 70772
(213) 555-7514
cgallo@rgwlaw.nita

COSME GALLO, JD

Education

Conwell University

- BA Political Science, YR-20
- Graduated summa cum laude
- Activities: Varsity Field Hockey, Student Government Representative

University of Nita School of Law

- JD, YR-17
- Graduated cum laude
- Activities: Mock Trial Competition Winner, Law Review
- Research Assistant—Professor John Wellman
- Assisted in updating THE NITA LAW OF PROFESSIONAL RESPONSIBILITY

Employment

YR-17–YR-14   Associate Counsel, Nita State Bar, Office of Disciplinary Counsel

- Responsible for investigating and prosecuting alleged violations of the Nita Code of Professional Responsibility.

YR-14–YR-11   Assistant District Attorney, Nita City Office of the District Attorney

- Investigated and prosecuted cases involving white collar crime.

YR-11–present   Partner, Roberts, Gallo & Wallach

- We are a twenty-four person law firm specializing in the litigation of plaintiff's personal injury and medical malpractice cases. In addition we handle white collar criminal defense cases.

Bar Memberships

- State of Nita
- Federal District Court
- U. S. Court of Appeals
- United States Supreme Court

Professional Association

- Nita State Bar Association
- Nita City Bar Association
- American Bar Association
- American Trial Lawyers Association

Expert Witness Testimony

In the past four years I have testified in eight professional negligence actions. My testimony was on behalf of Plaintiffs on two occasions and Defendants on six occasions. I provided deposition testimony in all eight cases and trial testimony in three cases.

DEPOSITION OF NOUR BASARA§§

My name is Nour Basara. I live at 27 Cable Court here in Nita City. I am a tenured full professor at the University of Nita School of Law. My qualifications are listed in my Rule 26 report and my resumé, which has been marked separately as EXHIBIT 2. I have been retained by the Nita State Bar to serve as an expert witness in the case of *In re Cooperman*. I have served this function more than twenty times in the past five years. It is true that each time I have testified for the State Bar, I have given the opinion that the charged lawyer violated the Nita Model Rules of Professional Conduct. In two situations, I was of the opinion that no violation occurred and did not testify. In fact, on both those occasions the State Bar dropped the matter.

My typical retainer for a matter such as this is $6,000, which is charged off at the rate of $350 per hour. I charge the same rate for my time, no matter what function I perform. That is, there is no premium hourly rate for courtroom testimony. In the typical case, my total fee averages between $5–$6,000. I also have served as an expert witness for plaintiffs in legal professional negligence cases. I have been retained in such matters approximately twenty-five times in the past four years. My fees are typically the same in malpractice cases as in disciplinary matters. Some of those retainers were in cases in which I also testified against the defendant lawyer in a disciplinary hearing. I am retained separately by plaintiff's counsel. That is because there is a different legal standard employed in legal malpractice than in disciplinary matters.

It is true that I earn a substantial amount of money as an expert witness. I would say my average annual income from my activities as an expert witness is approximately $75,000. I should point out that I have been offered retainers from defense lawyers in legal malpractice cases, but have declined them. It is very difficult for plaintiffs to find experts who are willing to testify against lawyers, so I feel a professional duty to make myself available to plaintiffs. This is so even though the defense work would probably be more lucrative, just judging on the amount of offers I have received.

My only other occupation is as a full time law professor. I do not actively engage in the practice of law, and haven't for many years. My active practice ended when I joined the law faculty in YR-16.

I do not know Ms. Cooperman, although I know of her work as a plaintiff's lawyer in the legal professional negligence area. No, I have never been hired by her as an expert witness. She has an excellent reputation as a lawyer who gets good results for her clients. To be candid, I was quite surprised when the State Bar approached me in this matter. I was disappointed when I found the violations that occurred during the course of her representation of Mr. Engels and Ms. Rubin. I agree that the violations here are by no means the most serious I have seen, but they are substantial.

To prepare myself for this opinion I have reviewed the charging papers, the depositions of Cooperman, Simpson, Engels, and Doran, relevant exhibits, and the applicable Model Rules of

---

§§ The transcript of Nour Basara's deposition was excerpted so that only the answers are reprinted here. Assume that this is a true and accurate rendering of those answers.

Professional Conduct. I have also consulted THE NITA LAW OF PROFESSIONAL RESPONSIBILITY by Professor John Wellman, who is a former colleague of mine. Professor Wellman retired from our faculty in YR-2, although he continues to update his treatise. It is an excellent book, although I have to say that I disagree with his interpretation of some of the rules, but that is to be expected among academics. I consider John to be a good friend. He was very helpful to me when I joined the law school faculty, especially after I chose to develop an expertise in Professional Responsibility.

In coming to my opinion I have assumed the following facts to be true. During the period of September YR-3–October YR-1, the respondent, Ms. Cooperman, represented Mr. Engels and Ms. Rubin in a personal injury matter arising out of a collision between a car driven by Rubin (in which Engels was a passenger) and a truck owned by the Acme Paper Company. The accident occurred because the truck turned left in front of the Rubin/Engels car, which had the right of way Although there was a distracting demonstration, the accident would not have happened without the failure of the Acme truck to yield the right of way. The demonstration was functionally irrelevant.

Respondent was approached by Engels and Rubin, who were seeking her representation. They were initially interviewed by Pat Simpson, a paralegal in respondent's office. Simpson learned that Engels was a passenger in Rubin's car and, quite accurately, recognized that Engels had a potential cause of action against Rubin as well as against the Acme Paper Company. After learning the identity of the potential defendant, Simpson explained to Engels that he could sue his friend, which he declined to do. Engels never understood from Simpson the full import of his claim against Rubin, nor the effect of his decision not to sue her. You are correct that nothing prevented him from asking questions about the impact of suing Rubin in his case, but that does not ameliorate the duty of a lawyer to fully explain any significant issue that arises in the litigation. The failure to consult effectively is at the core of the respondent's violation of the RPC.

Engels and Rubin were then interviewed by respondent.

Respondent has very little specific recollection of the interview, but based on her habit believes that she again went over the conflict between Engels and Rubin and explained the effect of the waiver. Again, the explanation, whatever it was, was not sufficient to impress upon Engels the import of his decision not to sue Rubin.

Engels and Rubin then retained respondent and signed a contingent fee agreement, which I have reviewed. (See EXHIBIT 4.) Respondent claims, again based on her habit and not specific recollection, that she went over the fee agreement with the clients. It is clear from Engels's deposition that although he may have understood the words of the agreement, he did not understand their import. You are correct; I find no evidence that Engels expressed a lack of understanding to the respondent.

The lawsuit was filed and the case proceeded in a fairly normal way. Respondent was difficult to contact by her clients, and often times did not return phone calls. In fact during the entire course of the representation, she met with Engels only at the initial interview, before the taking of his deposition, and at the two times that settlement was discussed. Virtually all other client contact was accomplished by the paralegal, Pat Simpson.

In the fall of YR-1 the defendant, Acme Paper Company, through its counsel, Jamie Doran, filed a motion to disqualify respondent due to an imputed conflict of interest. In YR-3, Acme Paper Company underwent a corporate reorganization, during which it was represented by a Ms. Matthews, who is a law partner of respondent. Although I have not spoken to her, I understand that during the course of that representation, Matthews was privy to confidential information regarding the full range of Acme's financial condition and policies. The motion claimed that, because Acme was a self-insurer, the information gathered in the former representation (and therefore the representation itself) was substantially related to the Engels and Rubin suit against Acme in that it would be helpful to determining the settlement posture of Acme in the Engels/Rubin litigation.

Ms. Cooperman was aware of the potential problem of representing clients in cases against former clients of the firm, and it had been discussed whether, in their conflicts search, paralegals should have available in the firm computer system a list of former clients and the nature of the former representation. Although this change to intake procedures had been discussed at the partner level, the system was not put in place until after this litigation was undertaken by the Board. (See Exhibits 7 and 8.)

Doran's motion was never decided because the case settled. In discussing the possibility of settlement, however, respondent did not mention the fact of the disqualification motion to her clients. Settlement offers were received that were substantially lower than what respondent led her clients to believe they would be.

Respondent then talked her clients into settling the case for these lower than expected amounts. The trial option was never really considered when discussing the settlement offers that were finally accepted.

The last interaction between respondent's law firm and Engels was at the time of the disbursal of proceeds of the settlement, which respondent did not attend. At that time, although surprised by the number and amount of the litigation costs, Engels signed the form presented to him and accepted his recovery check. (See Exhibit 6.) Shortly thereafter Engels made a complaint to the Nita State Bar that brought the instant case against respondent.

I am of the opinion that the respondent violated the Nita Model Rules of Professional Conduct in several respects. These violations, although committed knowingly, appear to be the result of a lack of attention to the important details of representing clients in a modern day practice, by a lawyer who was perhaps too busy to pay attention to those details. I will address the issues as denominated in the complaint filed by the Nita State Bar.

Count I charges respondent with failure to adequately consult with her client, so that the client could make informed decisions. This count of the complaint presents the overarching problem that exists in the representation of Engels and Rubin by the respondent. Rule 1.2(a) makes clear that the control over the objectives of a representation and means to be utilized in effectuating those objectives belongs to the client. Rule 1.4 requires that, in order to carry out the dictates of Rule 1.2 and the rest of the rules of professional conduct, it is incumbent upon the lawyer to regularly communicate with the client concerning those decisions that have to be made. In this representation, the respondent appears to have all but disregarded the dictates of these two rules.

The communication between respondent and her clients was sporadic at best. As mentioned earlier, there were only four occasions during the course of the almost two years of litigation when respondent even spoke with Mr. Engels: 1) at the time of the initial interview; 2) at the time of Engels's deposition; 3) before entering into settlement negotiations; and 4) when respondent sold her clients on the settlement. This pattern of behavior is at the root of all the problems in the representation. The specific failure to consult adequately will be addressed in the context of other violations of the rules, charged in Counts II, III, and IV.

The second count, although technical, is a prime example of a failure of the respondent to respond to the requirements of the rules. Rule 1.5(c) sets out a specific procedure for the creation of a contingent fee agreement between a lawyer and a client. In order that it be crystal clear what the amount of the fee will be, the rule requires a specific statement of the percentage of the fee as well as whether the fee is calculated before or after the expenses of the litigation are deducted. While it could be deduced from the contingent fee agreement that the fee was to be calculated before deducting the costs of the litigation by reading and interpreting several paragraphs, the rule (1.5) requires greater precision

All the respondent needed to do was to rewrite her standard contingent fee agreement in the express terms of the rule. Because she failed to do so and there is no evidence that she clearly explained the import of the fee agreement to her clients, we are left with precisely the situation the rule was designed to prevent; the client is unaware of the precise nature of the fee agreement.

In my opinion this rule is mandatory in its precision. This is an example of an area where I disagree with my good friend John Wellman. He would argue, I'm sure, that the rule need not be followed down to the wording, but rather that it must only be followed as to its intent. Although we disagree about the effect of the rule, in this case we would probably agree as to the result; this fee agreement, without clear and precise consultation, is violative of Rule 1.5(c). (See Exhibit 1.)

Count III charges the respondent with two violations of Rule 1.7. First, she is charged with the simultaneous representation of two clients with conflicting interests. This is probably the most serious of the charges against the respondent.

The respondent undertook the representation of Mr. Engels and Ms. Rubin in the cause of action arising out of the car accident between the Rubin car and the Acme truck. The cause of the accident was in dispute in that while the Acme truck turned left in front of the Rubin car and violated her right of way, Rubin was unable to avoid the accident because she was distracted by some demonstrators on the side of the street. No matter who caused the accident, Mr. Engels, a passenger in the Rubin car, was entitled, under the tort law of Nita, to full compensation for his injuries from either Rubin or Acme or, in all likelihood, both of them in relation to their respective negligence. For this reason, Engels and Rubin were in hopeless conflict.

Rule 1.7(a) provides: that a lawyer cannot represent both clients in such a situation unless first, the lawyer "reasonably believes that the lawyer will be able to provide competent and diligent representation to each affected client . . ." Rule 1.7 b(1). and second, having met the above requirement, "each affected client gives informed consent, confirmed in writing." Rule 1.7(b)(4). Respondent recognized that the conflict existed and apparently attempted to get the consent of both parties.

The problem here, however, is that the first clause of 1.7(a) cannot be met. This conflict is so basic that the representation of one client must always adversely affect the other. Engels, in order to protect his own interests, should sue both Acme and Rubin. If respondent represents Rubin, she cannot sue her on behalf of her other client Engels. As it turned out, the negligence of Rubin was very much in dispute in the lawsuit and even respondent admits that the negligence of Rubin, as argued by Acme's counsel, in part explains the low settlement offers. If respondent did not represent Rubin, this argument would have had no effect on the settlement for Engels. As a result, respondent should have made a claim on behalf of Engels against Rubin, but could not because of the joint representation, and therefore failed to meet Rule 1.7(b)(3).

Apparently respondent did not appreciate the proscription of rule 1.7(a)(1), nor appreciate the danger of undertaking the dual representation, as she did here, because she attempted to obtain a waiver of the conflict of interest. The conflict was recognized by respondent's paralegal, who attempted to consult with Engels. With all due respect to the talents of Pat Simpson, this consultation must be done by a lawyer and should not be done by a paralegal. This point is eloquently made by Professor Wellman in his treatise. (See Exhibit 9.)

Respondent has no recollection of consulting with Engels about the waiver and relies on her habit in explaining conflicts of interest to clients, generally, in testifying as to her "consultation" with Engels. In addition, she relies on the fee agreement with Engels, which contains a statement of the waiver of conflict of interest as well. (See Exhibit 4.) Again, respondent has no recollection of explaining the fee agreement, but merely states that she must have because of her habit of doing so. At bottom line, Engels, even given his intellect and education, did not understand what he was waiving. At a minimum, respondent should have explained that if Rubin was found to be 10 percent at fault for the accident, that the waiver had the effect of reducing Engel's collectable damages by 10 percent. This plainspoken kind of consultation is what is necessary when explaining the waiver of important rights.

The second part of Count III charges respondent with a conflict of interest between her client and herself. It is premised on the fact that Acme moved to disqualify respondent prior to the trial of the Engels and Rubin case. The motion was premised on another conflict of interest, which is charged in Count IV of the complaint. Suffice it to say, that if respondent were disqualified from the lawsuit, she would lose at least a portion of her fee. Respondent has stated that she did not place much weight on the motion, but that does not excuse her from consulting with her client about the conflict and obtaining a waiver as provided for in Rule 1.7(b).

Respondent failed to even mention the motion to disqualify when talking to her clients about the potential for settlement of the case. This failure of consultation presents a clear violation of both Rule 1.7 as well as Rule 1.4 regarding communication that was charged in Count I of the complaint. Although by no means certain from the facts of the case, this conflict may explain the further violation of Rules 1.2 and 1.4 committed by respondent when she did not adequately discuss the trial option with her clients. Obviously, the case could not be tried by respondent if she was disqualified.

Finally, Count IV of the complaint charges respondent with yet another conflict of interest based on the fact that another member of her firm had previously represented the Acme Paper Company in a corporate reorganization. This representation ended in the same year that respondent undertook the representation of Engels and Rubin against Acme. It is charged that this activity is violative of Rules 1.9 and 1.10 because the two representations were substantially related within the meaning of the rules.

At first blush it seems odd to claim that a corporate reorganization and automobile collision case are substantially related. In fact, because respondent's partner, Ms. Matthews, obtained confidential financial information from Acme, and because Acme is a self-insurer for automobile negligence cases, the former representation provided information that would be helpful to respondent in settling the case with Acme. This is so because ability to pay is always an issue in settlement, and knowing the financial condition of Acme can certainly by helpful in setting settlement values.

Respondent's position on this charge is that she and Ms. Matthews never communicated concerning Acme and therefore the information was of no use to her. This excuse is of no matter. Rule 1.10 imputes the knowledge of one partner (here Matthews) to her other partners, without requiring proof of actual sharing of confidences. The sharing of confidences in a law firm is presumed and cannot be overcome by mere testimony. Although this is a harsh rule, and one I've criticized in a University of Nita Law Review article published in YR-4 (See Exhibit 9), it is one well settled in the jurisprudence of this and most other jurisdictions, a fact that the article is careful to make.

It should be noted that the Cooperman and Jones firm has changed the conflicts check to now include former clients. I have two comments. First the check is for only five years previous to the new representation. I would recommend seven years as a more appropriate time. Second, the "new" contingent fee agreement seeks a waiver of the former client conflict from the client signing the contingent fee agreement. In actuality that waiver must be received from the former client.

In response to your question, I generally recognize John Wellman's treatise, The Nita Law Of Professional Responsibility, as an authoritative text on the law of professional responsibility, although I do disagree with certain sections of the work. Even as distinguished a man as John Wellman, who is a nationally known expert on professional responsibility, is not always correct on every issue.

I have read this deposition and it is complete and accurate.

[signature: Nour Basara]

_____

Nour Basara

This deposition was taken pursuant to an agreement between counsel to depose the expert witnesses in the case. It was taken in the office of the Respondent's counsel. The deposition was given under oath, and was read and signed by the deponent.

Subscribed and Sworn before me this 21st day of January, YR-0.

[signature: Harry Gibbons]

_____

Harry Gibbons
Certified Court Reporter

Exhibit 2

Nour Basara

3272 Michaelson Road, Grants River, Nita 57137   815.555.2938 ● nbasara@nitau.nita

EDUCATION	University of Nita, BA, Sociology, YR-23, magna cum laude
	
	University of Nita School of Law, JD, YR-20, summa cum laude
	    Activities: Editor in Chief—Law Review;
	    Phi Alpha Delta Legal Fraternity;
	    Student Bar Association Disciplinary Committee

EMPLOYMENT	Law Clerk, The Honorable Judith Jansen, Nita Supreme Court, YR-20–YR-19 Associate, Siler & Wright, Nita City, Nita Responsibilities: Worked primarily on corporate matters for Nita Power & Light Company and other public utilities, YR-19–YR-16 Associate Professor of Law, Nita University School of Law, YR-16–YR-11 Professor of Law, Nita University School of Law, YR-11–present
PUBLICATIONS	Basara, *Imputed Conflicts of Interest and the Modern Law Firm*, 54 U. Nita L. Rev. 417 (YR-4) Barasa, *The Plaintiff's Right to an Expert Witness in a Legal Malpractice Case*, 48 Nita Bar Journal 1 (YR-7) Basara, *Towards a National Standard for Legal Malpractice*, 46 Conwell L. Rev. 76 (YR-11) Basara and Wallace, *Cases and Problems in Business Associations*, Nita Press (YR-12) Basara, *Business Torts: The Case against the Company*, 45 U. Nita L. Rev. 111 (YR-13) Basara, *Insider Trading and Corporate Counsel*, 17 Nita Corp. L. Rev. 24 (YR-15)
COURSES TAUGHT	Business Associations Legal Malpractice (Seminar) Professional Responsibility Torts
BAR MEMBERSHIPS	State of Nita U.S. District Court for the Eastern District of Nita U.S. Court of Appeals for the 12th Circuit U.S. Supreme Court

CONSULTING

In the past four years I have served as an expert witness and testified in a variety of legal professional negligence and professional disciplinary charges. My testimony has been at deposition in eighteen cases, four of which went to a trial or hearing where I testified as well. In all cases I have testified that professional negligence or a violation of the MRPC had occurred. I have been qualified as an expert witness on legal malpractice and professional responsibility in the state and federal courts of Nita as well as before Nita State Disciplinary Board.

Exhibit 3

Excerpts from Wellman's The Nita Law of Professional Responsibility

Chapter III—Beginning the Attorney Client Relationship, Section 5, Page 98

Once it has been determined that the client's lawsuit will be handled on a contingent fee basis, Nita Model Rule 1.5(c) provides that the agreement must be in writing. The rule, when read in its entirety, expresses the concern that the client fully understands the amount of the fee by understanding how the fee will be calculated and whether the attorney or client will be responsible for paying the costs of the litigation. This can be easily accomplished by drafting a contingent fee agreement that tracks the rule literally. The rule does not, however, require such a stilted contractual form. So long as the agreement makes clear the percentage of the award or settlement that will be the attorney's fee, and whether the attorney or client will be responsible for the costs of litigation, the contract will pass professional responsibility muster. As always when dealing with an important matter with a client, the fee agreement should be gone over with the client to reasonably assure client understanding. Special care should be taken when dealing with a client who is uneducated or has difficulty in comprehending such matters.

Chapter VI—Conflicts of Interest, Section 8, Page 323

One final word about obtaining a waiver of a conflict of interest. Conflicts of interest are perhaps the most complicated of all professional responsibility matters for clients to comprehend. As we have seen, they often involve complicated legal premises and an ethical system that is unknown to other professions. As a result, the waiver of a conflict should be carefully and precisely handled by the attorney who seeks it. This matter should not be handled as a matter of rote, nor should it be handled by such nonprofessionals as office administrators, paralegals, or secretaries. In addition, whenever a client waives a conflict of interest, it should be memorialized in some sort of writing that is affirmed by the client.

Exhibit 4

COOPERMAN & JONES

A Professional Corporation
1201 Market Street NITA CITY, NITA 99996 (721) 555-5010

CONTINGENT FEE AGREEMENT

I hereby retain the law firm of Cooperman & Jones to represent me with respect to all injuries that I suffered arising out of an automobile collision with a truck owned by the ACME PAPER COMPANY and driven by WALTER BREWER on or about JANUARY 6, YR-4.

I agree that I will pay as fee for services rendered a sum equal to thirty three and one-third percent (33 1/3%) of the total amount of any recovery on my behalf, by way of settlement of verdict.

I agree that I am responsible for all reasonable and necessary costs and expenses incurred in the investigation and prosecution of this claim.

I further understand and agree that by this agreement, Cooperman & Jones is not committed in any way to proceed with a lawsuit and have the right at any time to determine that it is not appropriate for them to continue to handle my case.

Should the case be pursued to its conclusion by Cooperman & Jones, I understand that all reasonable and necessary expenses must be paid by me, regardless of the outcome of the case.

WAIVER

I further understand that I have a potential cause of action against MARY RUBIN arising out of an automobile collision that occurred on or about JANUARY 6, YR-4. After being fully informed of the impact of my decision, I hereby waive my right to bring such lawsuit, and further waive any potential conflict of interest between MARY RUBIN and myself that would preclude representation of me in this cause of action by Cooperman & Jones. I understand that no settlement of the claim will be consummated without my prior approval.

I have read and understand the above one (1) page agreement and hereby acknowledge the receipt of a duplicate copy of this Contingent Fee Agreement.

_____
DAVID ENGELS
Date: September 8, YR-3

Witness: _____
HARRIET COOPERMAN

Exhibit 5

COOPERMAN & JONES

Harriet Cooperman

David Engels — 28K - 11K - 100K

Mary Rubin — 6K - 1.6K - 20-25K

Defendant:

   ACME PAPER

   W. BREWER (Driver)

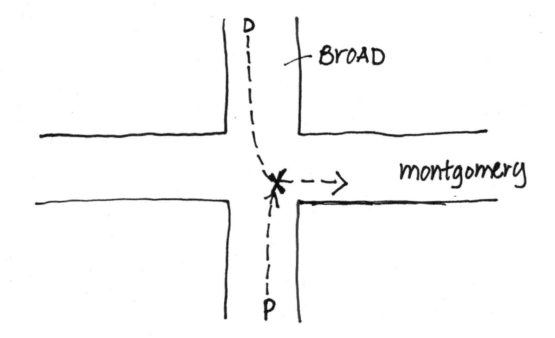

Conflict-OK

Exhibit 6

COOPERMAN & JONES

A Professional Corporation
1201 MARKET STREET NITA CITY, NITA 99996 (721) 555-5010

October 10, YR-1

Mr. David Engels
17 Oak Ridge Lane
Nita City, Nita
Account # 1-447-3

Re: ENGELS v. ACME PAPER COMPANY

Disbursal of Settlement

Total Settlement $70,000.00

Deductions

Professional Fee	$23,100.00
Filing Fees	150.00
Court Reporter Fees	1,100.00
Copying	45.40
Client Lunch	18.50
Cab Fare	12.00
Expert Witness Fees	3,000.00
Total Deductions	$27,425.90

Net to Client $42,574.10

I hereby acknowledge receipt of a check in the amount of $42,574.10 and agree that it is the full amount due and owing me in the matter of ENGELS v. ACME PAPER COMPANY.

David Engels
_____
DAVID ENGELS
October 10, YR-1

Witness: _Pat Simpson_
_____
PAT SIMPSON

Exhibit 7

Harriet Cooperman

From:	Harriet Cooperman <hcooperman@coopermanjones.nita>
Sent:	January 14, Yr-0
To:	**Company Wide**
Subject:	Intake Procedures
Attachments:	CONTINGENT_FEE_AGREEMENT

As you know we have solicited from all of you over the past few months ways in which we can improve our intake procedures to protect ourselves from unintended errors or misinformation to our clients. Until now, we have conducted a computer search of current clients only to determine if there is a conflict of interest.

As our firm has grown and we have two separate sections of the firm, we have not taken into account conflicts that might occur with former clients of our firm. This is the subject of current frivolous charge brought against Harriet by the NITA Disciplinary Board, where all allegations are meritless. The charges do point out that there is a possibility that there can exist a potential conflict between a potential new client and a former client if the representation of the former client is substantially related to the new client's potential matter.

To that end, we now have available on our computer system a listing of all former clients. Paralegals are instructed that when they discover a situation where a potential new client is suing a former client, to look further into the former representation (which is available on our expanded system to make a preliminary determination when the former representation and the potential new representation are substantially related.) The paralegal must note that potential conflict to the lawyer in charge of the case who is to make an independent determination as to whether there is a substantial relationship between the former representation and the potential client. In most cases this will be an easy decision. It is an unusual case where we will have a former client with a matter substantially related to a new client. If the lawyer in charge of the case believes that there is no conflict, the search and the decision should be noted in the file, explained to the client and our retainer agreement should reflect the waiver by the client. In that case the enclosed retainer form should be utilized.

Exhibit 8

COOPERMAN & JONES

A Professional Corporation
1201 Market Street NITA CITY, NITA 99996 (721) 555-5010

CONTINGENT FEE AGREEMENT

I hereby retain the law firm of Cooperman & Jones to represent me with respect to all injuries that I suffered_____

I agree that I will pay as fee for services rendered a sum equal to thirty three and one-third percent (33 1/3%) of the total amount of any recovery on my behalf, by way of settlement of verdict. t.

I agree that I am responsible for all reasonable and necessary costs and expenses incurred in the investigation and prosecution of this claim.

I further understand and agree that by this agreement, Cooperman & Jones is not committed in any way to proceed with a lawsuit and has the right at any time to determine that it is not appropriate for them to continue to handle my case.

Should the case be pursued to its conclusion by Cooperman & Jones, I understand that all reasonable and necessary expenses must be paid by me, regardless of the outcome of the case.

WAIVER

I understand that I have a potential cause of action against arising out of an automobile collision that occurred on or about_____. After being fully informed of the impact of my decision, I hereby waive my right to bring such lawsuit, and further waive any potential conflict of interest between _____ and myself that would preclude representation of me in this cause of action by Cooperman & Jones. I understand that no settlement of the claim will be consummated without my prior approval.

I further understand that there was a potential conflict between this matter and a previous matter handled by Cooperman & Jones, which my lawyer has explained to me and advised that it is not operative.

I have read and understand the above one (1) page agreement and hereby acknowledge the receipt of a duplicate copy of this Contingent Fee Agreement.

Client: _____   Witness: _____

Date: _____

Exhibit 9

Excerpt from Nita Law Review Article

There exists in the Model Rules a provision that the information of one partner is imputed to all of the partners in the firm. In the days of small firms this rule was appropriate and probably accurate. In meetings the partners could review the facts of the cases they were working on which would alert a partner with information from a previous representation that might create a conflict. That imputation of knowledge is unreasonable in modern day practice where law firms often operate in different sections (e.g., Litigation, Commercial, Tax, Bankruptcy, etc.) and it is unrealistic that the information of one partner is in fact known to other partners. The rule, therefore, should require before there is a conflict based on information obtained in a previous law suit, that the partner in the new matter must have **<u>actual</u> knowledge** of the information from the previous matter in the firm.

Basara, *Imputed Conflict of Interest and the Modern Law Firm*, 54 U. Nita L. Rev, 417, 433, Yr-4.

Texts between Cooperman and Jones
Regarding Conflicts of Interest

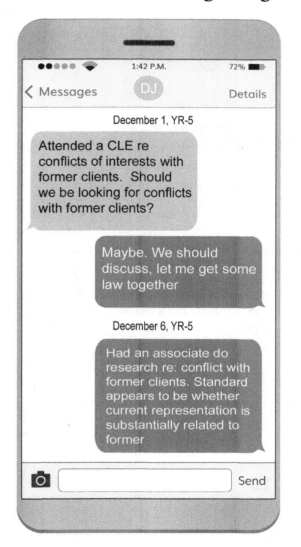

Exhibit 10B

January 12, YR-2

Did you see the article re: client conflict in The Intelligencer?

No. Must have missed it.

Firm about our size got sued for conflict with former client.

That's not good

Maybe time to revisit this issue. Expand our database to include former clients.

This will be a big project, digging up that info.

I know. Time to finally update the computers. I think we need 5 years of clients.

The staff will be happy with new equipment. Some of the info will be in archives, but it will all have to be updated

People move, businesses change names. This is going to be labor intensive.

APPENDIX

American Bar Association Model Rules of Professional Conduct

Adopted August 1983, as Amended to August 2002.

Excerpted from the *Model Rules of Professional Conduct,*
copyright by the American Bar Association.
All rights reserved. Reprinted with permission.

PREAMBLE, SCOPE, AND TERMINOLOGY

Preamble: A Lawyer's Responsibilities

A lawyer, as a member of the legal profession, is a representative of clients, an officer of the legal system and a public citizen having special responsibility for the quality of justice.

As a representative of clients, a lawyer performs various functions. As advisor, a lawyer provides a client with an informed understanding of the client's legal rights and obligations and explains their practical implications. As advocate, a lawyer zealously asserts the client's position under the rules of the adversary system. As negotiator, a lawyer seeks a result advantageous to the client but consistent with requirements of honest dealings with others. As an evaluator, a lawyer acts by examining a client's legal affairs and reporting about them to the client or to others.

In addition to these representational functions, a lawyer may serve as a third-party neutral, a nonrepresentational role helping the parties to resolve a dispute or other matter. Some of these Rules apply directly to lawyers who are or have served as third-party neutrals. See, e.g., Rules 1.12 and 2.4. In addition, there are Rules that apply to lawyers who are not active in the practice of law or to practicing lawyers even when they are acting in a nonprofessional capacity. For example, a lawyer who commits fraud in the conduct of a business is subject to discipline for engaging in conduct involving dishonesty, fraud, deceit or misrepresentation. See Rule 8.4.

In all professional functions a lawyer should be competent, prompt and diligent. A lawyer should maintain communication with a client concerning the representation. A lawyer should keep in confidence information relating to representation of a client except so far as disclosure is required or permitted by the Rules of Professional Conduct or other law.

A lawyer's conduct should conform to the requirements of the law, both in professional service to clients and in the lawyer's business and personal affairs. A lawyer should use the law's procedures only for legitimate purposes and not to harass or intimidate others. A lawyer should demonstrate respect for the legal system and for those who serve it, including judges, other lawyers and public officials. While it is a lawyer's duty, when necessary, to challenge the rectitude of official action, it is also a lawyer's duty to uphold legal process.

As a public citizen, a lawyer should seek improvement of the law, access to the legal system, the administration of justice and the quality of service rendered by the legal profession. As a member of a learned profession, a lawyer should cultivate knowledge of the law beyond its use for clients, employ that knowledge in reform of the law and work to strengthen legal education. In addition, a lawyer should further the public's understanding of and confidence in the rule of law and the justice system because legal institutions in a constitutional democracy depend on popular participation and support to maintain their authority. A lawyer should be mindful of deficiencies in the administration of justice and of the fact that the poor, and sometimes persons who are not poor, cannot afford adequate legal assistance. Therefore, all lawyers should devote professional time and resources and use civic influence to ensure equal access to our system of justice for all those who because of economic or social barriers cannot afford or secure adequate legal counsel. A lawyer should aid the legal profession in pursuing these objectives and should help the bar regulate itself in the public interest.

Many of a lawyer's professional responsibilities are prescribed in the Rules of Professional Conduct, as well as substantive and procedural law. However, a lawyer is also guided by personal conscience and the approbation of professional peers. A lawyer should strive to attain the highest level of skill, to improve the law and the legal profession and to exemplify the legal profession's ideals of public service.

A lawyer's responsibilities as a representative of clients, an officer of the legal system and a public citizen are usually harmonious. Thus, when an opposing party is well represented, a lawyer can be a zealous advocate on behalf of a client and at the same time assume that justice is being done. So also, a lawyer can be sure that preserving client confidences ordinarily serves the public interest because people are more likely to seek legal advice, and thereby heed their legal obligations, when they know their communications will be private.

In the nature of law practice, however, conflicting responsibilities are encountered. Virtually all difficult ethical problems arise from conflict between a lawyer's responsibilities to clients, to the legal system and to the lawyer's own interest in remaining an ethical person while earning a satisfactory living. The Rules of Professional Conduct often prescribe terms for resolving such conflicts. Within the framework of these Rules, however, many difficult issues of professional discretion can arise. Such issues must be resolved through the exercise of sensitive professional and moral judgment guided by the basic principles underlying the Rules. These principles include the lawyer's obligation zealously to protect and pursue a client's legitimate interests, within the bounds of the law, while maintaining a professional, courteous and civil attitude toward all persons involved in the legal system.

The legal profession is largely self-governing. Although other professions also have been granted powers of self-government, the legal profession is unique in this respect because of the close relationship between the profession and the processes of government and law enforcement. This connection is manifested in the fact that ultimate authority over the legal profession is vested largely in the courts.

To the extent that lawyers meet the obligations of their professional calling, the occasion for government regulation is obviated. Self-regulation also helps maintain the legal profession's independence from government domination. An independent legal profession is an important force in preserving government under law, for abuse of legal authority is more readily challenged by a profession whose members are not dependent on government for the right to practice.

The legal profession's relative autonomy carries with it special responsibilities of self-government. The profession has a responsibility to assure that its regulations are conceived in the public interest and not in furtherance of parochial or self-interested concerns of the bar. Every lawyer is responsible for observance of the Rules of Professional Conduct. A lawyer should also aid in securing their observance by other lawyers. Neglect of these responsibilities compromises the independence of the profession and the public interest which it serves.

Lawyers play a vital role in the preservation of society. The fulfillment of this role requires an understanding by lawyers of their relationship to our legal system. The Rules of Professional Conduct, when properly applied, serve to define that relationship.

Scope

The Rules of Professional Conduct are rules of reason. They should be interpreted with reference to the purposes of legal representation and of the law itself. Some of the Rules are imperatives, cast in the terms "shall" or "shall not." These define proper conduct for purposes of professional discipline. Others, generally cast in the term "may," are permissive and define areas under the Rules in which the lawyer has discretion to exercise professional judgment. No disciplinary action should be taken when the lawyer chooses not to act or acts within the bounds of such discretion. Other Rules define the nature of relationships between the lawyer and others. The Rules are thus partly obligatory and disciplinary and partly constitutive and descriptive in that they define a lawyer's professional role. Many of the Comments use the term "should." Comments do not add obligations to the Rules but provide guidance for practicing in compliance with the Rules.

The Rules presuppose a larger legal context shaping the lawyer's role. That context includes court rules and statutes relating to matters of licensure, laws defining specific obligations of lawyers and substantive and procedural law in general. The Comments are sometimes used to alert lawyers to their responsibilities under such other law.

Compliance with the Rules, as with all law in an open society, depends primarily upon understanding and voluntary compliance, secondarily upon reinforcement by peer and public opinion and finally, when necessary, upon enforcement through disciplinary proceedings. The Rules do not, however, exhaust the moral and ethical considerations that should inform a lawyer, for no worthwhile human activity can be completely defined by legal rules. The Rules simply provide a framework for the ethical practice of law.

Furthermore, for purposes of determining the lawyer's authority and responsibility, principles of substantive law external to these Rules determine whether a client-lawyer relationship exists. Most of the duties flowing from the client-lawyer relationship attach only after the client has requested the lawyer to render legal services and the lawyer has agreed to do so. But there are some duties, such as that of confidentiality under Rule 1.6, that attach when the lawyer agrees to consider whether a client-lawyer relationship shall be established. See Rule 1.18. Whether a client-lawyer relationship exists for any specific purpose can depend on the circumstances and may be a question of fact.

Under various legal provisions, including constitutional, statutory and common law, the responsibilities of government lawyers may include authority concerning legal matters that ordinarily reposes in the client in private client-lawyer relationships. For example, a lawyer for a government agency may have authority on behalf of the government to decide upon settlement or whether to appeal from an adverse judgment. Such authority in various respects is generally vested in the attorney general and the state's attorney in state government, and their federal counterparts, and the same may be true of other government law officers. Also, lawyers under the supervision of these officers may be authorized to represent several government agencies in intragovernmental legal controversies in circumstances where a private lawyer could not represent multiple private clients. These Rules do not abrogate any such authority.

Failure to comply with an obligation or prohibition imposed by a Rule is a basis for invoking the disciplinary process. The Rules presuppose that disciplinary assessment of a lawyer's conduct will be made on the basis of the facts and circumstances as they existed at the time of the conduct in question and in recognition of the fact that a lawyer often has to act upon uncertain or incomplete evidence of the situation. Moreover, the Rules presuppose that whether or not discipline should be imposed for a violation, and the severity of a sanction, depend on all the circumstances, such as the willfulness and seriousness of the violation, extenuating factors and whether there have been previous violations.

Violation of a Rule should not itself give rise to a cause of action against a lawyer nor should it create any presumption in such a case that a legal duty has been breached. In addition, violation of a Rule does not necessarily warrant any other nondisciplinary remedy, such as disqualification of a lawyer in pending litigation. The Rules are designed to provide guidance to lawyers and to provide a structure for regulating conduct through disciplinary agencies. They are not designed to be a basis for civil liability. Furthermore, the purpose of the Rules can be subverted when they are invoked by opposing parties as procedural weapons. The fact that a Rule is a just basis for a lawyer's self-assessment, or for sanctioning a lawyer under the administration of a disciplinary authority, does not imply that an antagonist in a collateral proceeding or transaction has standing to seek enforcement of the Rule. Nevertheless, since the Rules do establish standards of conduct by lawyers, a lawyer's violation of a Rule may be evidence of breach of the applicable standard of conduct.

The Comment accompanying each Rule explains and illustrates the meaning and purpose of the Rule. The Preamble and this note on Scope provide general orientation. The Comments are intended as guides to interpretation, but the text of each Rule is authoritative.

RULE 1.0 Terminology

"Belief" or "believes" denotes that the person involved actually supposed the fact in question to be true. A person's belief may be inferred from circumstances.

"Confirmed in writing," when used in reference to the informed consent of a person, denotes informed consent that is given in writing by the person or a writing that a lawyer promptly transmits to the person confirming an oral informed consent. See paragraph (e) for the definition of "informed consent." If it is not feasible to obtain or transmit the writing at the time the person gives informed consent, then the lawyer must obtain or transmit it within a reasonable time thereafter.

"Firm" or "law firm" denotes a lawyer or lawyers in a law partnership, professional corporation, sole proprietorship or other association authorized to practice law; or lawyers employed in a legal services organization or the legal department of a corporation or other organization.

"Fraud" or "fraudulent" denotes conduct that is fraudulent under the substantive or procedural law of the applicable jurisdiction and has a purpose to deceive.

"Informed consent" denotes the agreement by a person to a proposed course of conduct after the lawyer has communicated adequate information and explanation about the material risks of and reasonably available alternatives to the proposed course of conduct.

"Knowingly," "known," or "knows" denotes actual knowledge of the fact in question. A person's knowledge may be inferred from circumstances.

"Partner" denotes a member of a partnership, a shareholder in a law firm organized as a professional corporation, or a member of an association authorized to practice law.

"Reasonable" or "reasonably" when used in relation to conduct by a lawyer denotes the conduct of a reasonably prudent and competent lawyer.

"Reasonable belief" or "reasonably believes" when used in reference to a lawyer denotes that the lawyer believes the matter in question and that the circumstances are such that the belief is reasonable.

"Reasonably should know" when used in reference to a lawyer denotes that a lawyer of reasonable prudence and competence would ascertain the matter in question.

"Screened" denotes the isolation of a lawyer from any participation in a matter through the timely imposition of procedures within a firm that are reasonably adequate under the circumstances to protect information that the isolated lawyer is obligated to protect under these Rules or other law.

"Substantial" when used in reference to degree or extent denotes a material matter of clear and weighty importance.

"Tribunal" denotes a court, an arbitrator in a binding arbitration proceeding or a legislative body, administrative agency or other body acting in an adjudicative capacity. A legislative body, administrative agency or other body acts in an adjudicative capacity when a neutral official, after the presentation of evidence or legal argument by a party or parties, will render a binding legal judgment directly affecting a party's interests in a particular matter.

"Writing" or "written" denotes a tangible or electronic record of a communication or representation, including handwriting, typewriting, printing, photostating, photography, audio or videorecording and email. A "signed" writing includes an electronic sound, symbol or process attached to or logically associated with a writing and executed or adopted by a person with the intent to sign the writing.

RULE 1.2 Scope of Representation and Allocation of Authority Between Client and Lawyer

(a) Subject to paragraphs (c) and (d), a lawyer shall abide by a client's decisions concerning the objectives of representation and, as required by Rule 1.4, shall consult with the client as to the means by which they are to be pursued. A lawyer may take such action on behalf of the client as is impliedly authorized to carry out the representation. A lawyer shall abide by a client's decision whether to settle a matter. In a criminal case, the lawyer shall abide by the client's decision, after consultation with the lawyer, as to a plea to be entered, whether to waive jury trial and whether the client will testify.

(b) A lawyer's representation of a client, including representation by appointment, does not constitute an endorsement of the client's political, economic, social or moral views or activities.

(c) A lawyer may limit the scope of the representation if the limitation is reasonable under the circumstances and the client gives informed consent.

(d) A lawyer shall not counsel a client to engage, or assist a client, in conduct that the lawyer knows is criminal or fraudulent, but a lawyer may discuss the legal consequences of any proposed course of conduct with a client and may counsel or assist a client to make a good faith effort to determine the validity, scope, meaning or application of the law.

Comment:

Paragraph (a) confers upon the client the ultimate authority to determine the purposes to be served by legal representation, within the limits imposed by law and the lawyer's professional obligations. The decisions specified in paragraph (a), such as whether to settle a civil matter, must also be made by the client. See Rule 1.4(a)(1) for the lawyer's duty to communicate with the client about such decisions. With respect to the means by which the client's objectives are to be pursued, the lawyer shall consult with the client as required by Rule 1.4(a)(2) and may take such action as is impliedly authorized to carry out the representation.

On occasion, however, a lawyer and a client may disagree about the means to be used to accomplish the client's objectives. Clients normally defer to the special knowledge and skill of their lawyer with respect to the means to be used to accomplish their objectives, particularly with respect to technical, legal and tactical matters. Conversely, lawyers usually defer to the client regarding such questions as the expense to be incurred and concern for third persons who might be adversely affected. Because of the varied nature of the matters about which a lawyer and client might disagree and because the actions in question may implicate the interests of a tribunal or other persons, this Rule does not prescribe how such disagreements are to be resolved. Other law, however, may be applicable and should be consulted by the lawyer. The lawyer should also consult with the client and seek a mutually acceptable resolution of the disagreement. If such efforts are unavailing and the lawyer has a fundamental disagreement with the client, the lawyer may withdraw from the representation. See Rule 1.16(b)(4). Conversely, the client may resolve the disagreement by discharging the lawyer. See Rule 1.16(a)(3).

At the outset of a representation, the client may authorize the lawyer to take specific action on the client's behalf without further consultation. Absent a material change in circumstances and subject to Rule 1.4, a lawyer may rely on such an advance authorization. The client may, however, revoke such authority at any time.

In a case in which the client appears to be suffering diminished capacity, the lawyer's duty to abide by the client's decisions is to be guided by reference to Rule 1.14.

Independence from Client's Views or Activities

Legal representation should not be denied to people who are unable to afford legal services, or whose cause is controversial or the subject of popular disapproval. By the same token, representing a client does not constitute approval of the client's views or activities.

Agreements Limiting Scope of Representation

The scope of services to be provided by a lawyer may be limited by agreement with the client or by the terms under which the lawyer's services are made available to the client. When a lawyer has been retained by an insurer to represent an insured, for example, the representation may be limited to matters related to the insurance coverage. A limited representation may be appropriate because the client has limited objectives for the representation. In addition, the terms upon which representation is undertaken may exclude specific means that might otherwise be used to accomplish the client's objectives. Such limitations may exclude actions that the client thinks are too costly or that the lawyer regards as repugnant or imprudent.

Although this Rule affords the lawyer and client substantial latitude to limit the representation, the limitation must be reasonable under the circumstances. If, for example, a client's objective is limited to securing general information about the law the client needs in order to handle a common and typically uncomplicated legal problem, the lawyer and client may agree that the lawyer's services will be limited to a brief telephone consultation. Such a limitation, however, would not be reasonable if the time allotted was not sufficient to yield advice upon which the client could rely. Although an agreement for a limited representation does not exempt a lawyer from the duty to provide competent representation, the limitation is a factor to be considered when determining the legal knowledge, skill, thoroughness and preparation reasonably necessary for the representation. See Rule 1.1.

All agreements concerning a lawyer's representation of a client must accord with the Rules of Professional Conduct and other law. See, e.g., Rules 1.1, 1.8 and 5.6.

Criminal, Fraudulent and Prohibited Transactions

Paragraph (d) prohibits a lawyer from knowingly counseling or assisting a client to commit a crime or fraud. This prohibition, however, does not preclude the lawyer from giving an honest opinion about the actual consequences that appear likely to result from a client's conduct. Nor does the fact that a client uses advice in a course of action that is criminal or fraudulent of itself make a lawyer a party to the course of action. There is a critical distinction between presenting an analysis of legal aspects of questionable conduct and recommending the means by which a crime or fraud might be committed with impunity.

When the client's course of action has already begun and is continuing, the lawyer's responsibility is especially delicate. The lawyer is required to avoid assisting the client, for example, by drafting or delivering documents that the lawyer knows are fraudulent or by suggesting how the wrongdoing might be concealed. A lawyer may not continue assisting a client in conduct that the lawyer originally supposed was legally proper but then discovers is criminal or fraudulent. The lawyer must, therefore, withdraw from the representation of the client in the matter. See Rule 1.16(a). In some cases, withdrawal alone might be insufficient. It may be necessary for the lawyer to give notice of the fact of withdrawal and to disaffirm any opinion, document, affirmation or the like. See Rule 4.1.

Where the client is a fiduciary, the lawyer may be charged with special obligations in dealings with a beneficiary.

Paragraph (d) applies whether or not the defrauded party is a party to the transaction. Hence, a lawyer must not participate in a transaction to effectuate criminal or fraudulent avoidance of tax liability. Paragraph (d) does not preclude undertaking a criminal defense incident to a general retainer for legal services to a lawful enterprise. The last clause of paragraph (d) recognizes that determining the validity or interpretation of a statute or regulation may require a course of action involving disobedience of the statute or regulation or of the interpretation placed upon it by governmental authorities.

If a lawyer comes to know or reasonably should know that a client expects assistance not permitted by the Rules of Professional Conduct or other law or if the lawyer intends to act contrary to the client's instructions, the lawyer must consult with the client regarding the limitations on the lawyer's conduct. See Rule 1.4(a)(5).

RULE 1.4 Communication

(a) A lawyer shall:

(1) promptly inform the client of any decision or circumstance with respect to which the client's informed consent, as defined in Rule 1.0(e), is required by these Rules;

(2) reasonably consult with the client about the means by which the client's objectives are to be accomplished;

(3) keep the client reasonably informed about the status of the matter;

(4) promptly comply with reasonable requests for information; and

(5) consult with the client about any relevant limitation on the lawyer's conduct when the lawyer knows that the client expects assistance not permitted by the Rules of Professional Conduct or other law.

(b) A lawyer shall explain a matter to the extent reasonably necessary to permit the client to make informed decisions regarding the representation.

Comment:

Reasonable communication between the lawyer and the client is necessary for the client effectively to participate in the representation.

Communicating with Client

If these Rules require that a particular decision about the representation be made by the client, paragraph (a)(1) requires that the lawyer promptly consult with and secure the client's consent prior to taking action unless prior discussions with the client have resolved what action the client wants the lawyer to take. For example, a lawyer who receives from opposing counsel an offer of settlement in a civil controversy or a proffered plea bargain in a criminal case must promptly inform the client of its substance unless the client has previously indicated that the proposal will be acceptable or unacceptable or has authorized the lawyer to accept or to reject the offer. See Rule 1.2(a).

Paragraph (a)(2) requires the lawyer to reasonably consult with the client about the means to be used to accomplish the client's objectives. In some situations—depending on both the importance of the action under consideration and the feasibility of consulting with the client—this duty will require consultation prior to taking action. In other circumstances, such as during a trial when an immediate decision must be made, the exigency of the situation may require the lawyer to act without prior consultation. In such cases the lawyer must nonetheless act reasonably to inform the client of actions the lawyer has taken on the client's behalf. Additionally, paragraph (a)(3) requires that the lawyer keep the client reasonably informed about the status of the matter, such as significant developments affecting the timing or the substance of the representation.

A lawyer's regular communication with clients will minimize the occasions on which a client will need to request information concerning the representation. When a client makes a reasonable request for information, however, paragraph (a)(4) requires prompt compliance with the request, or if a prompt response is not feasible, that the lawyer, or a member of the lawyer's staff, acknowledge receipt of the request and advise the client when a response may be expected. Client telephone calls should be promptly returned or acknowledged.

Explaining Matters

The client should have sufficient information to participate intelligently in decisions concerning the objectives of the representation and the means by which they are to be pursued, to the extent the client is willing and able to do so. Adequacy of communication depends in part on the kind of advice or assistance that is involved. For example, when there is time to explain a proposal made in a negotiation, the lawyer should review all important provisions with the client before proceeding to an agreement. In litigation a lawyer should explain the general strategy and prospects of success and ordinarily should consult the client on tactics that are likely to result in significant expense or to injure or coerce others. On the other hand, a lawyer ordinarily will not be expected to describe trial or negotiation strategy in detail. The guiding principle is that the lawyer should fulfill reasonable client expectations for information consistent with the duty to act in the client's best interests, and the client's overall requirements as to the character of representation. In certain circumstances, such as when a lawyer asks a client to consent to a representation affected by a conflict of interest, the client must give informed consent, as defined in Rule 1.0(e).

Ordinarily, the information to be provided is that appropriate for a client who is a comprehending and responsible adult. However, fully informing the client according to this standard may be impracticable, for example, where the client is a child or suffers from diminished capacity. See Rule 1.14. When the client is an organization or group, it is often impossible or inappropriate to inform every one of its members about its legal affairs; ordinarily, the lawyer should address communications to the appropriate officials of the organization. See Rule 1.13. Where many routine matters are involved, a system of limited or occasional reporting may be arranged with the client.

Withholding Information

In some circumstances, a lawyer may be justified in delaying transmission of information when the client would be likely to react imprudently to an immediate communication. Thus, a lawyer might withhold a psychiatric diagnosis of a client when the examining psychiatrist indicates that disclosure would harm the client. A lawyer may not withhold information to serve the lawyer's own interest or convenience or the interests or convenience of another person. Rules or court orders governing litigation may provide that information supplied to a lawyer may not be disclosed to the client. Rule 3.4(c) directs compliance with such rules or orders.

RULE 1.5 Fees

(a) A lawyer shall not make an agreement for, charge, or collect an unreasonable fee or an unreasonable amount for expenses. The factors to be considered in determining the reasonableness of a fee include the following:

    (1) the time and labor required, the novelty and difficulty of the questions involved, and the skill requisite to perform the legal service properly;

    (2) the likelihood, if apparent to the client, that the acceptance of the particular employment will preclude other employment by the lawyer;

    (3) the fee customarily charged in the locality for similar legal services;

    (4) the amount involved and the results obtained;

    (5) the time limitations imposed by the client or by the circumstances;

    (6) the nature and length of the professional relationship with the client;

    (7) the experience, reputation, and ability of the lawyer or lawyers performing the services; and

    (8) whether the fee is fixed or contingent.

(b) The scope of the representation and the basis or rate of the fee and expenses for which the client will be responsible shall be communicated to the client, preferably in writing, before or within a reasonable time after commencing the representation, except when the lawyer will charge a regularly represented client on the same basis or rate. Any changes in the basis or rate of the fee or expenses shall also be communicated to the client.

(c) A fee may be contingent on the outcome of the matter for which the service is rendered, except in a matter in which a contingent fee is prohibited by paragraph (d) or other law. A contingent fee agreement shall be in a writing signed by the client and shall state the method by which the fee is to be determined, including the percentage or percentages that shall accrue to the lawyer in the event of settlement, trial or appeal; litigation and other expenses to be deducted from the recovery; and whether such expenses are to be deducted before or after the contingent fee is calculated. The agreement must clearly notify the client of any expenses for which the client will be liable whether or not the client is the prevailing party. Upon conclusion of a contingent fee matter, the lawyer shall provide the client with a written statement stating the outcome of the matter and, if there is a recovery, showing the remittance to the client and the method of its determination.

(d) A lawyer shall not enter into an arrangement for, charge, or collect:

(1) any fee in a domestic relations matter, the payment or amount of which is contingent upon the securing of a divorce or upon the amount of alimony or support, or property settlement in lieu thereof; or

(2) a contingent fee for representing a defendant in a criminal case.

(e) A division of a fee between lawyers who are not in the same firm may be made only if:

(1) the division is in proportion to the services performed by each lawyer or each lawyer assumes joint responsibility for the representation;

(2) the client agrees to the arrangement, including the share each lawyer will receive, and the agreement is confirmed in writing; and

(3) the total fee is reasonable.

Comment:

Reasonableness of Fee and Expenses

Paragraph (a) requires that lawyers charge fees that are reasonable under the circumstances. The factors specified in (1) through (8) are not exclusive. Nor will each factor be relevant in each instance. Paragraph (a) also requires that expenses for which the client will be charged must be reasonable. A lawyer may seek reimbursement for the cost of services performed in-house, such as copying, or for other expenses incurred in-house, such as telephone charges, either by charging a reasonable amount to which the client has agreed in advance or by charging an amount that reasonably reflects the cost incurred by the lawyer.

Basis or Rate of Fee

When the lawyer has regularly represented a client, they ordinarily will have evolved an understanding concerning the basis or rate of the fee and the expenses for which the client will be responsible. In a new client-lawyer relationship, however, an understanding as to fees and expenses must be promptly established. Generally, it is desirable to furnish the client with at least a simple memorandum or copy of the lawyer's customary fee arrangements that states the general nature of the legal services to be provided, the basis, rate or total amount of the fee and whether and to what extent the client will be responsible for any costs, expenses or disbursements in the course of the representation. A written statement concerning the terms of the engagement reduces the possibility of misunderstanding.

Contingent fees, like any other fees, are subject to the reasonableness standard of paragraph (a) of this Rule. In determining whether a particular contingent fee is reasonable, or whether it is reasonable to charge any form of contingent fee, a lawyer must consider the factors that are relevant under the circumstances. Applicable law may impose limitations on contingent fees, such as a ceiling on the percentage allowable, or may require a lawyer to offer clients an alternative basis for the fee. Applicable law also may apply to situations other than a contingent fee, for example, government regulations regarding fees in certain tax matters.

Terms of Payment

A lawyer may require advance payment of a fee, but is obliged to return any unearned portion. See Rule 1.16(d). A lawyer may accept property in payment for services, such as an ownership interest in an enterprise, providing this does not involve acquisition of a proprietary interest in the cause of action or subject matter of the litigation contrary to Rule 1.8 (i). However, a fee paid in property instead of money may be subject to the requirements of Rule 1.8(a) because such fees often have the essential qualities of a business transaction with the client.

An agreement may not be made whose terms might induce the lawyer improperly to curtail services for the client or perform them in a way contrary to the client's interest. For example, a lawyer should not enter into an agreement whereby services are to be provided only up to a stated amount when it is foreseeable that more extensive services probably will be required, unless the situation is adequately explained to the client. Otherwise, the client might have to bargain for further assistance in the midst of a proceeding or transaction. However, it is proper to define the extent of services in light of the client's ability to pay. A lawyer should not exploit a fee arrangement based primarily on hourly charges by using wasteful procedures.

Prohibited Contingent Fees

Paragraph (d) prohibits a lawyer from charging a contingent fee in a domestic relations matter when payment is contingent upon the securing of a divorce or upon the amount of alimony or support or property settlement to be obtained. This provision does not preclude a contract for a contingent fee for legal representation in connection with the recovery of post-judgment balances due under support, alimony or other financial orders because such contracts do not implicate the same policy concerns.

Division of Fee

A division of fee is a single billing to a client covering the fee of two or more lawyers who are not in the same firm. A division of fee facilitates association of more than one lawyer in a matter in which neither alone could serve the client as well, and most often is used when the fee is contingent and the division is between a referring lawyer and a trial specialist. Paragraph (e) permits the lawyers to divide a fee either on the basis of the proportion of services they render or if each lawyer assumes responsibility for the representation as a whole. In addition, the client must agree to the arrangement, including the share that each lawyer is to receive, and the agreement must be confirmed in writing. Contingent fee agreements must be in a writing signed by the client and must otherwise comply with paragraph (c) of this Rule. Joint responsibility for the representation entails financial and ethical responsibility for the representation as if the lawyers were associated in a partnership. A lawyer should only refer a matter to a lawyer whom the referring lawyer reasonably believes is competent to handle the matter. See Rule 1.1.

Paragraph (e) does not prohibit or regulate division of fees to be received in the future for work done when lawyers were previously associated in a law firm.

Disputes over Fees

If a procedure has been established for resolution of fee disputes, such as an arbitration or mediation procedure established by the bar, the lawyer must comply with the procedure when it is mandatory, and, even when it is voluntary, the lawyer should conscientiously consider submitting to it. Law may prescribe a procedure for determining a lawyer's fee, for example, in representation of an executor or administrator, a class or a person entitled to a reasonable fee as part of the measure of damages. The lawyer entitled to such a fee and a lawyer representing another party concerned with the fee should comply with the prescribed procedure.

RULE 1.7 Conflict of Interest: Current Clients

(a) Except as provided in paragraph (b), a lawyer shall not represent a client if the representation involves a concurrent conflict of interest. A concurrent conflict of interest exists if:

    (1) the representation of one client will be directly adverse to another client; or

    (2) there is a significant risk that the representation of one or more clients will be materially limited by the lawyer's responsibilities to another client, a former client or a third person or by a personal interest of the lawyer.

(b) Notwithstanding the existence of a concurrent conflict of interest under paragraph (a), a lawyer may represent a client if:

    (1) the lawyer reasonably believes that the lawyer will be able to provide competent and diligent representation to each affected client;

    (2) the representation is not prohibited by law;

    (3) the representation does not involve the assertion of a claim by one client against another client represented by the lawyer in the same litigation or other proceeding before a tribunal; and

    (4) each affected client gives informed consent, confirmed in writing.

Comment: General Principles

Loyalty and independent judgment are essential elements in the lawyer's relationship to a client. Concurrent conflicts of interest can arise from the lawyer's responsibilities to another client, a former client or a third person or from the lawyer's own interests. For specific Rules regarding certain concurrent conflicts of interest, see Rule 1.8. For former client conflicts of interest, see Rule 1.9. For conflicts of interest involving prospective clients, see Rule 1.18. For definitions of "informed consent" and "confirmed in writing," see Rule 1.0(e) and (b).

Resolution of a conflict of interest problem under this Rule requires the lawyer to: 1) clearly identify the client or clients; 2) determine whether a conflict of interest exists; 3) decide whether the representation may be undertaken despite the existence of a conflict, i.e., whether the conflict is consentable; and 4) if so, consult with the clients affected under paragraph (a) and obtain their informed consent, confirmed in writing. The clients affected under paragraph (a) include both of the clients referred to in paragraph (a)(1) and the one or more clients whose representation might be materially limited under paragraph (a)(2).

A conflict of interest may exist before representation is undertaken, in which event the representation must be declined, unless the lawyer obtains the informed consent of each client under the conditions of paragraph (b). To determine whether a conflict of interest exists, a lawyer should adopt reasonable procedures, appropriate for the size and type of firm and practice, to determine in both litigation and non-litigation matters the persons and issues involved. See also Comment to Rule 5.1. Ignorance caused by a failure to institute such procedures will not excuse a lawyer's violation of this Rule. As to whether a client-lawyer relationship exists or, having once been established, is continuing, see Comment to Rule 1.3 and Scope.

If a conflict arises after representation has been undertaken, the lawyer ordinarily must withdraw from the representation, unless the lawyer has obtained the informed consent of the client under the conditions of paragraph (b). See Rule 1.16. Where more than one client is involved, whether the lawyer may continue to represent any of the clients is determined both by the lawyer's ability to comply with duties owed to the former client and by the lawyer's ability to represent adequately the remaining client or clients, given the lawyer's duties to the former client. See Rule 1.9. See also Comments [5] and [29].

Unforeseeable developments, such as changes in corporate and other organizational affiliations or the addition or realignment of parties in litigation, might create conflicts in the midst of a representation, as when a company sued by the lawyer on behalf of one client is bought by another client represented by the lawyer in an unrelated matter. Depending on the circumstances, the lawyer may have the option to withdraw from one of the representations in order to avoid the conflict. The lawyer must seek court approval where necessary and take steps to minimize harm to the clients. See Rule 1.16. The lawyer must continue to protect the confidences of the client from whose representation the lawyer has withdrawn. See Rule 1.9(c).

Identifying Conflicts of Interest: Directly Adverse

Loyalty to a current client prohibits undertaking representation directly adverse to that client without that client's informed consent. Thus, absent consent, a lawyer may not act as an advocate in one matter against a person the lawyer represents in some other matter, even when the matters are wholly unrelated. The client as to whom the representation is directly adverse is likely to feel betrayed, and the resulting damage to the client-lawyer relationship is likely to impair the lawyer's ability to represent the client effectively. In addition, the client on whose behalf the adverse representation is undertaken reasonably may fear that the lawyer will pursue that client's case less effectively out of deference to the other client, i.e., that the representation may be materially limited by the lawyer's interest in retaining the current client. Similarly, a directly adverse conflict may arise when a lawyer is required to cross-examine a client who appears as a witness in a lawsuit involving another client, as when the testimony will be damaging to the client who is represented in the lawsuit. On the other hand, simultaneous representation in unrelated matters of clients whose interests are only economically adverse, such as representation of competing economic enterprises in unrelated litigation, does not ordinarily constitute a conflict of interest and thus may not require consent of the respective clients.

Directly adverse conflicts can also arise in transactional matters. For example, if a lawyer is asked to represent the seller of a business in negotiations with a buyer represented by the lawyer, not in the same transaction but in another, unrelated matter, the lawyer could not undertake the representation without the informed consent of each client.

Identifying Conflicts of Interest: Material Limitation

Even where there is no direct adverseness, a conflict of interest exists if there is a significant risk that a lawyer's ability to consider, recommend or carry out an appropriate course of action for the client will be materially limited as a result of the lawyer's other responsibilities or interests. For example, a lawyer asked to represent several individuals seeking to form a joint venture is likely to be materially limited in the lawyer's ability to recommend or advocate all possible positions that each might take because of the lawyer's duty of loyalty to the others. The conflict in effect forecloses alternatives that would otherwise be available to the client. The mere possibility of subsequent harm does not itself require disclosure and consent. The critical questions are the likelihood that a difference in interests will eventuate and, if it does, whether it will materially interfere with the lawyer's independent professional judgment in considering alternatives or foreclose courses of action that reasonably should be pursued on behalf of the client.

Lawyer's Responsibilities to Former Clients and Other Third Persons

In addition to conflicts with other current clients, a lawyer's duties of loyalty and independence may be materially limited by responsibilities to former clients under Rule 1.9 or by the lawyer's responsibilities to other persons, such as fiduciary duties arising from a lawyer's service as a trustee, executor or corporate director.

Personal Interest Conflicts

The lawyer's own interests should not be permitted to have an adverse effect on representation of a client. For example, if the probity of a lawyer's own conduct in a transaction is in serious question, it may be difficult or impossible for the lawyer to give a client detached advice. Similarly, when a lawyer has discussions concerning possible employment with an opponent of the lawyer's client, or with a law firm representing the opponent, such discussions could materially limit the lawyer's representation of the client. In addition, a lawyer may not allow related business interests to affect representation, for example, by referring clients to an enterprise in which the lawyer has an undisclosed financial interest. See Rule 1.8 for specific Rules pertaining to a number of personal interest conflicts, including business transactions with clients. See also Rule 1.10 (personal interest conflicts under Rule 1.7 ordinarily are not imputed to other lawyers in a law firm).

When lawyers representing different clients in the same matter or in substantially related matters are closely related by blood or marriage, there may be a significant risk that client confidences will be revealed and that the lawyer's family relationship will interfere with both loyalty and independent professional judgment. As a result, each client is entitled to know of the existence and implications of the relationship between the lawyers before the lawyer agrees to undertake the representation. Thus, a lawyer related to another lawyer, e.g., as parent, child, sibling or spouse, ordinarily may not represent a client in a matter where that lawyer is representing another party, unless each client gives informed consent. The disqualification arising from a close family relationship is personal and ordinarily is not imputed to members of firms with whom the lawyers are associated. See Rule 1.10.

A lawyer is prohibited from engaging in sexual relationships with a client unless the sexual relationship predates the formation of the client-lawyer relationship. See Rule 1.8(j).

Interest of Person Paying for a Lawyer's Service

A lawyer may be paid from a source other than the client, including a co-client, if the client is informed of that fact and consents and the arrangement does not compromise the lawyer's duty of loyalty or independent judgment to the client. See Rule 1.8(f). If acceptance of the payment from any other source presents a significant risk that the lawyer's representation of the client will be materially limited by the lawyer's own interest in accommodating the person paying the lawyer's fee or by the lawyer's responsibilities to a payer who is also a co-client, then the lawyer must comply with the requirements of paragraph (b) before accepting the representation, including determining whether the conflict is consentable and, if so, that the client has adequate information about the material risks of the representation.

Prohibited Representations

Ordinarily, clients may consent to representation notwithstanding a conflict. However, as indicated in paragraph (b), some conflicts are nonconsentable, meaning that the lawyer involved cannot properly ask for such agreement or provide representation on the basis of the client's consent. When the lawyer is representing more than one client, the question of consentability must be resolved as to each client.

Consentability is typically determined by considering whether the interests of the clients will be adequately protected if the clients are permitted to give their informed consent to representation burdened by a conflict of interest. Thus, under paragraph (b)(1), representation is prohibited if in the circumstances the lawyer cannot reasonably conclude that the lawyer will be able to provide competent and diligent representation. See Rule 1.1 (competence) and Rule 1.3 (diligence).

Paragraph (b)(2) describes conflicts that are nonconsentable because the representation is prohibited by applicable law. For example, in some states substantive law provides that the same lawyer may not represent more than one defendant in a capital case, even with the consent of the clients, and under federal criminal statutes certain representations by a former government lawyer are prohibited, despite the informed consent of the former client. In addition, decisional law in some states limits the ability of a governmental client, such as a municipality, to consent to a conflict of interest.

Paragraph (b)(3) describes conflicts that are nonconsentable because of the institutional interest in vigorous development of each client's position when the clients are aligned directly against each other in the same litigation or other proceeding before a tribunal. Whether clients are aligned directly against each other within the meaning of this paragraph requires examination of the context of the proceeding. Although this paragraph does not preclude a lawyer's multiple representation of adverse parties to a mediation (because mediation is not a proceeding before a "tribunal" under Rule 1.0(m)), such representation may be precluded by paragraph (b)(1).

Informed Consent

Informed consent requires that each affected client be aware of the relevant circumstances and of the material and reasonably foreseeable ways that the conflict could have adverse effects on the interests of that client. See Rule 1.0(e) (informed consent). The information required depends on the nature of the conflict and the nature of the risks involved. When representation of multiple clients in a single matter is undertaken, the information must include the implications of the common representation, including possible effects on loyalty, confidentiality and the attorney-client privilege and the advantages and risks involved. See Comments [30] and [31] (effect of common representation on confidentiality).

Under some circumstances it may be impossible to make the disclosure necessary to obtain consent. For example, when the lawyer represents different clients in related matters and one of the clients refuses to consent to the disclosure necessary to permit the other client to make an informed decision, the lawyer cannot properly ask the latter to consent. In some cases the alternative to common representation can be that each party may have to obtain separate representation with the possibility of incurring additional costs. These costs, along with the benefits of securing separate representation, are factors that may be considered by the affected client in determining whether common representation is in the client's interests.

Consent Confirmed in Writing

Paragraph (b) requires the lawyer to obtain the informed consent of the client, confirmed in writing. Such a writing may consist of a document executed by the client or one that the lawyer promptly records and transmits to the client following an oral consent. See Rule 1.0(b). See also Rule 1.0(n) (writing includes electronic transmission). If it is not feasible to obtain or transmit the writing at the time the client gives informed consent, then the lawyer must obtain or transmit it within a reasonable time thereafter. See Rule 1.0(b). The requirement of a writing does not supplant the need in most cases for the lawyer to talk with the client, to explain the risks and advantages, if any, of representation burdened with a conflict of interest, as well as reasonably available alternatives, and to afford the client a reasonable opportunity to consider the risks and alternatives and to raise questions and concerns. Rather, the writing is required in order to impress upon clients the seriousness of the decision the client is being asked to make and to avoid disputes or ambiguities that might later occur in the absence of a writing.

Revoking Consent

A client who has given consent to a conflict may revoke the consent and, like any other client, may terminate the lawyer's representation at any time. Whether revoking consent to the client's own representation precludes the lawyer from continuing to represent other clients depends on the circumstances, including the nature of the conflict, whether the client revoked consent because of a material change in circumstances, the reasonable expectations of the other client and whether material detriment to the other clients or the lawyer would result.

Consent to Future Conflict

Whether a lawyer may properly request a client to waive conflicts that might arise in the future is subject to the test of paragraph (b). The effectiveness of such waivers is generally determined by the extent to which the client reasonably understands the material risks that the waiver entails. The more comprehensive the explanation of the types of future representations that might arise and the actual and reasonably foreseeable adverse consequences of those representations, the greater the likelihood that the client will have the requisite understanding. Thus, if the client agrees to consent to a particular type of conflict with which the client is already familiar, then the consent ordinarily will be effective with regard to that type of conflict. If the consent is general and open-ended, then the consent ordinarily will be ineffective, because it is not reasonably likely that the client will have understood the material risks involved. On the other hand, if the client is an experienced user of the legal services involved and is reasonably informed regarding the risk that a conflict may arise, such consent is more likely to be effective, particularly if, e.g., the client is independently represented by other counsel in giving consent and the consent is limited to future conflicts unrelated to the subject of the representation. In any case, advance consent cannot be effective if the circumstances that materialize in the future are such as would make the conflict nonconsentable under paragraph (b).

Conflicts in Litigation

Paragraph (b)(3) prohibits representation of opposing parties in the same litigation, regardless of the clients' consent. On the other hand, simultaneous representation of parties whose interests in litigation may conflict, such as coplaintiffs or codefendants, is governed by paragraph (a)(2). A conflict may exist by reason of substantial discrepancy in the parties' testimony, incompatibility in positions in relation to an opposing party or the fact that there are substantially different possibilities of settlement of the claims or liabilities in question. Such conflicts can arise in criminal cases as well as civil. The potential for conflict of interest in representing multiple defendants in a criminal case is so grave that ordinarily a lawyer should decline to represent more than one codefendant. On the other hand, common representation of persons having similar interests in civil litigation is proper if the requirements of paragraph (b) are met.

Ordinarily a lawyer may take inconsistent legal positions in different tribunals at different times on behalf of different clients. The mere fact that advocating a legal position on behalf of one client might create precedent adverse to the interests of a client represented by the lawyer in an unrelated matter does not create a conflict of interest. A conflict of interest exists, however, if there is a significant risk that a lawyer's action on behalf of one client will materially limit the lawyer's effectiveness in representing another client in a different case; for example, when a decision favoring one client will create a precedent likely to seriously weaken the position taken on behalf of the other client. Factors relevant in determining whether the clients need to be advised of the risk include: where the cases are pending, whether the issue is substantive or procedural, the temporal relationship between the matters, the significance of the issue to the immediate and long-term interests of the clients involved and the clients' reasonable expectations in retaining the lawyer. If there is significant risk of material limitation, then absent informed consent of the affected clients, the lawyer must refuse one of the representations or withdraw from one or both matters.

When a lawyer represents or seeks to represent a class of plaintiffs or defendants in a class-action lawsuit, unnamed members of the class are ordinarily not considered to be clients of the lawyer for purposes of applying paragraph (a)(1) of this Rule. Thus, the lawyer does not typically need to get the consent of such a person before representing a client suing the person in an unrelated matter. Similarly, a lawyer seeking to represent an opponent in a class action does not typically need the consent of an unnamed member of the class whom the lawyer represents in an unrelated matter.

Nonlitigation Conflicts

Conflicts of interest under paragraphs (a)(1) and (a)(2) arise in contexts other than litigation. For a discussion of directly adverse conflicts in transactional matters, see Comment [7]. Relevant factors in determining whether there is significant potential for material limitation include the duration and intimacy of the lawyer's relationship with the client or clients involved, the functions being performed by the lawyer, the likelihood that disagreements will arise and the likely prejudice to the client from the conflict. The question is often one of proximity and degree. See Comment [8].

For example, conflict questions may arise in estate planning and estate administration. A lawyer may be called upon to prepare wills for several family members, such as husband and wife, and, depending upon the circumstances, a conflict of interest may be present. In estate administration the identity of the client may be unclear under the law of a particular jurisdiction. Under one view, the client is the fiduciary; under another view the client is the estate or trust, including its beneficiaries. In order to comply with conflict of interest rules, the lawyer should make clear the lawyer's relationship to the parties involved.

Whether a conflict is consentable depends on the circumstances. For example, a lawyer may not represent multiple parties to a negotiation whose interests are fundamentally antagonistic to each other, but common representation is permissible where the clients are generally aligned in interest even though there is some difference in interest among them. Thus, a lawyer may seek to establish or adjust a relationship between clients on an amicable and mutually advantageous basis; for example, in helping to organize a business in which two or more clients are entrepreneurs, working out the financial reorganization of an enterprise in which two or more clients have an interest or arranging a property distribution in settlement of an estate. The lawyer seeks to resolve potentially adverse interests by developing the parties' mutual interests. Otherwise, each party might have to obtain separate representation, with the possibility of incurring additional cost, complication or even litigation. Given these and other relevant factors, the clients may prefer that the lawyer act for all of them.

Special Considerations in Common Representation

In considering whether to represent multiple clients in the same matter, a lawyer should be mindful that if the common representation fails because the potentially adverse interests cannot be reconciled, the result can be additional cost, embarrassment and recrimination. Ordinarily, the lawyer will be forced to withdraw from representing all of the clients if the common representation fails. In some situations, the risk of failure is so great that multiple representation is plainly impossible. For example, a lawyer cannot undertake common representation of clients where contentious litigation or negotiations between them are imminent or contemplated. Moreover, because the lawyer is required to be impartial between commonly represented clients, representation of multiple clients is improper when it is unlikely that impartiality can be maintained. Generally, if the relationship between the parties has already assumed antagonism, the possibility that the clients' interests can be adequately served by common representation is not very good. Other relevant factors are whether the lawyer subsequently will represent both parties on a continuing basis and whether the situation involves creating or terminating a relationship between the parties.

A particularly important factor in determining the appropriateness of common representation is the effect on client-lawyer confidentiality and the attorney-client privilege. With regard to the attorney-client privilege, the prevailing rule is that, as between commonly represented clients, the privilege does not attach. Hence, it must be assumed that if litigation eventuates between the clients, the privilege will not protect any such communications, and the clients should be so advised.

As to the duty of confidentiality, continued common representation will almost certainly be inadequate if one client asks the lawyer not to disclose to the other client information relevant to the common representation. This is so because the lawyer has an equal duty of loyalty to each client, and each client has the right to be informed of anything bearing on the representation that might affect that client's interests and the right to expect that the lawyer will use that information to that client's benefit. See Rule 1.4. The lawyer should, at the outset of the common representation and as part of the process of obtaining each client's informed consent, advise each client that information will be shared and that the lawyer will have to withdraw if one client decides that some matter material to the representation should be kept from the other. In limited circumstances, it may be appropriate for the lawyer to proceed with the representation when the clients have agreed, after being properly informed, that the lawyer will keep certain information confidential. For example, the lawyer may reasonably conclude that failure to disclose one client's trade secrets to another client will not adversely affect representation involving a joint venture between the clients and agree to keep that information confidential with the informed consent of both clients.

When seeking to establish or adjust a relationship between clients, the lawyer should make clear that the lawyer's role is not that of partisanship normally expected in other circumstances and, thus, that the clients may be required to assume greater responsibility for decisions than when each client is separately represented. Any limitations on the scope of the representation made necessary as a result of the common representation should be fully explained to the clients at the outset of the representation. See Rule 1.2(c).

Subject to the above limitations, each client in the common representation has the right to loyal and diligent representation and the protection of Rule 1.9 concerning the obligations to a former client. The client also has the right to discharge the lawyer as stated in Rule 1.16.

Organizational Clients

A lawyer who represents a corporation or other organization does not, by virtue of that representation, necessarily represent any constituent or affiliated organization, such as a parent or subsidiary. See Rule 1.13(a). Thus, the lawyer for an organization is not barred from accepting representation adverse to an affiliate in an unrelated matter, unless the circumstances are such that the affiliate should also be considered a client of the lawyer, there is an understanding between the lawyer and the organizational client that the lawyer will avoid representation adverse to the client's affiliates, or the lawyer's obligations to either the organizational client or the new client are likely to limit materially the lawyer's representation of the other client.

A lawyer for a corporation or other organization who is also a member of its board of directors should determine whether the responsibilities of the two roles may conflict. The lawyer may be called on to advise the corporation in matters involving actions of the directors. Consideration should be given to the frequency with which such situations may arise, the potential intensity of the conflict, the effect of the lawyer's resignation from the board and the possibility of the corporation's obtaining legal advice from another lawyer in such situations. If there is material risk that the dual role will compromise the lawyer's independence of professional judgment, the lawyer should not serve as a director or should cease to act as the corporation's lawyer when conflicts of interest arise. The lawyer should advise the other members of the board that in some circumstances matters discussed at board meetings while the lawyer is present in the capacity of director might not be protected by the attorney-client privilege and that conflict of interest considerations might require the lawyer's recusal as a director or might require the lawyer and the lawyer's firm to decline representation of the corporation in a matter.

RULE 1.9 Duties to Former Client

(a) A lawyer who has formerly represented a client in a matter shall not thereafter represent another person in the same or a substantially related matter in which that person's interests are materially adverse to the interests of the former client unless the former client gives informed consent, confirmed in writing.

(b) A lawyer shall not knowingly represent a person in the same or a substantially related matter in which a firm with which the lawyer formerly was associated had previously represented a client

   (1) whose interests are materially adverse to that person; and

   (2) about whom the lawyer had acquired information protected by Rules 1.6 and 1.9(c) that is material to the matter;

   unless the former client gives informed consent, confirmed in writing.

(c) A lawyer who has formerly represented a client in a matter or whose present or former firm has formerly represented a client in a matter shall not thereafter:

   (1) use information relating to the representation to the disadvantage of the former client except as these Rules would permit or require with respect to a client, or when the information has become generally known; or

   (2) reveal information relating to the representation except as these Rules would permit or require with respect to a client.

Comment:

After termination of a client-lawyer relationship, a lawyer has certain continuing duties with respect to confidentiality and conflicts of interest and thus may not represent another client except in conformity with this Rule. Under this Rule, for example, a lawyer could not properly seek to rescind on behalf of a new client a contract drafted on behalf of the former client. So also a lawyer who has prosecuted an accused person could not properly represent the accused in a subsequent civil action against the government concerning the same transaction. Nor could a lawyer who has represented multiple clients in a matter represent one of the clients against the others in the same or a substantially related matter after a dispute arose among the clients in that matter, unless all affected clients give informed consent. See Comment [9]. Current and former government lawyers must comply with this Rule to the extent required by Rule 1.11.

The scope of a "matter" for purposes of this Rule depends on the facts of a particular situation or transaction. The lawyer's involvement in a matter can also be a question of degree. When a lawyer has been directly involved in a specific transaction, subsequent representation of other clients with materially adverse interests in that transaction clearly is prohibited. On the other hand, a lawyer who recurrently handled a type of problem for a former client is not precluded from later representing another client in a factually distinct problem of that type even though the subsequent representation involves a position adverse to the prior client. Similar considerations can apply to the reassignment of military lawyers between defense and prosecution functions within the same military jurisdictions. The underlying question is whether the lawyer was so involved in the matter that the subsequent representation can be justly regarded as a changing of sides in the matter in question.

Matters are "substantially related" for purposes of this Rule if they involve the same transaction or legal dispute or if there otherwise is a substantial risk that confidential factual information as would normally have been obtained in the prior representation would materially advance the client's position in the subsequent matter. For example, a lawyer who has represented a businessperson and learned extensive private financial information about that person may not then represent that person's spouse in seeking a divorce. Similarly, a lawyer who has previously represented a client in securing environmental permits to build a shopping center would be precluded from representing neighbors seeking to oppose rezoning of the property on the basis of environmental considerations; however, the lawyer would not be precluded, on the grounds of substantial relationship, from defending a tenant of the completed shopping center in resisting eviction for nonpayment of rent. Information that has been disclosed to the public or to other parties adverse to the former client ordinarily will not be disqualifying. Information acquired in a prior representation may have been rendered obsolete by the passage of time, a circumstance that may be relevant in determining whether two representations are substantially related. In the case of an organizational client, general knowledge of the client's policies and practices ordinarily will not preclude a subsequent representation; on the other hand, knowledge of specific facts gained in a prior representation that are relevant to the matter in question ordinarily will preclude such a representation. A former client is not required to reveal the confidential information learned by the lawyer in order to establish a substantial risk that the lawyer has confidential information to use in the subsequent matter. A conclusion about the possession of such information may be based on the nature of the services the lawyer provided the former client and information that would in ordinary practice be learned by a lawyer providing such services.

Lawyers Moving Between Firms

When lawyers have been associated within a firm but then end their association, the question of whether a lawyer should undertake representation is more complicated. There are several competing considerations. First, the client previously represented by the former firm must be reasonably assured that the principle of loyalty to the client is not compromised. Second, the rule should not be so broadly cast as to preclude other persons from having reasonable choice of legal counsel. Third, the rule should not unreasonably hamper lawyers from forming new associations and taking on new clients after having left a previous association. In this connection, it should be recognized that today many lawyers practice in firms, that many lawyers to some degree limit their practice to one field or another, and that many move from one association to another several times in their careers. If the concept of imputation were applied with unqualified rigor, the result would be radical curtailment of the opportunity of lawyers to move from one practice setting to another and of the opportunity of clients to change counsel.

Paragraph (b) operates to disqualify the lawyer only when the lawyer involved has actual knowledge of information protected by Rules 1.6 and 1.9(c). Thus, if a lawyer while with one firm acquired no knowledge or information relating to a particular client of the firm, and that lawyer later joined another firm, neither the lawyer individually nor the second firm is disqualified from representing another client in the same or a related matter even though the interests of the two clients conflict. See Rule 1.10(b) for the restrictions on a firm once a lawyer has terminated association with the firm.

Application of paragraph (b) depends on a situation's particular facts, aided by inferences, deductions or working presumptions that reasonably may be made about the way in which lawyers work together. A lawyer may have general access to files of all clients of a law firm and may regularly participate in discussions of their affairs; it should be inferred that such a lawyer in fact is privy to all information about all the firm's clients. In contrast, another lawyer may have access to the files of only a limited number of clients and participate in discussions of the affairs of no other clients; in the absence of information to the contrary, it should be inferred that such a lawyer in fact is privy to information about the clients actually served but not those of other clients. In such an inquiry, the burden of proof should rest upon the firm whose disqualification is sought.

Independent of the question of disqualification of a firm, a lawyer changing professional association has a continuing duty to preserve confidentiality of information about a client formerly represented. See Rules 1.6 and 1.9(c).

Paragraph (c) provides that information acquired by the lawyer in the course of representing a client may not subsequently be used or revealed by the lawyer to the disadvantage of the client. However, the fact that a lawyer has once served a client does not preclude the lawyer from using generally known information about that client when later representing another client.

The provisions of this Rule are for the protection of former clients and can be waived if the client gives informed consent, which consent must be confirmed in writing under paragraphs (a) and (b). See Rule 1.0(e). With regard to the effectiveness of an advance waiver, see Comment [22] to Rule 1.7. With regard to disqualification of a firm with which a lawyer is or was formerly associated, see Rule 1.10.

RULE 1.10 Imputed of Conflicts of Interest: General Rule

(a) While lawyers are associated in a firm, none of them shall knowingly represent a client when any one of them practicing alone would be prohibited from doing so by Rules 1.7 or 1.9, unless the prohibition is based on a personal interest of the prohibited lawyer and does not present a significant risk of materially limiting the representation of the client by the remaining lawyers in the firm.

(b) When a lawyer has terminated an association with a firm, the firm is not prohibited from thereafter representing a person with interests materially adverse to those of a client represented by the formerly associated lawyer and not currently represented by the firm, unless:

(1) the matter is the same or substantially related to that in which the formerly associated lawyer represented the client; and

(2) any lawyer remaining in the firm has information protected by Rules 1.6 and 1.9(c) that is material to the matter.

(c) A disqualification prescribed by this rule may be waived by the affected client under the conditions stated in Rule 1.7.

(d) The disqualification of lawyers associated in a firm with former or current government lawyers is governed by Rule 1.11.

Comment:

Definition of "Firm"

For purposes of the Rules of Professional Conduct, the term "firm" denotes lawyers in a law partnership, professional corporation, sole proprietorship or other association authorized to practice law; or lawyers employed in a legal services organization or the legal department of a corporation or other organization. See Rule 1.0(c). Whether two or more lawyers constitute a firm within this definition can depend on the specific facts. See Rule 1.0, Comments [2]–[4].

Principles of Imputed Disqualification

The rule of imputed disqualification stated in paragraph (a) gives effect to the principle of loyalty to the client as it applies to lawyers who practice in a law firm. Such situations can be considered from the premise that a firm of lawyers is essentially one lawyer for purposes of the rules governing loyalty to the client, or from the premise that each lawyer is vicariously bound by the obligation of loyalty owed by each lawyer with whom the lawyer is associated. Paragraph (a) operates only among the lawyers currently associated in a firm. When a lawyer moves from one firm to another, the situation is governed by Rules 1.9(b) and 1.10(b).

The rule in paragraph (a) does not prohibit representation where neither questions of client loyalty nor protection of confidential information are presented. Where one lawyer in a firm could not effectively represent a given client because of strong political beliefs, for example, but that lawyer will do no work on the case and the personal beliefs of the lawyer will not materially limit the representation by others in the firm, the firm should not be disqualified. On the other hand, if an opposing party in a case were owned by a lawyer in the law firm, and others in the firm would be materially limited in pursuing the matter because of loyalty to that lawyer, the personal disqualification of the lawyer would be imputed to all others in the firm.

The rule in paragraph (a) also does not prohibit representation by others in the law firm where the person prohibited from involvement in a matter is a nonlawyer, such as a paralegal or legal secretary. Nor does paragraph (a) prohibit representation if the lawyer is prohibited from acting because of events before the person became a lawyer, for example, work that the person did while a law student. Such persons, however, ordinarily must be screened from any personal participation in the matter to avoid communication to others in the firm of confidential information that both the nonlawyers and the firm have a legal duty to protect. See Rules 1.0(k) and 5.3.

Rule 1.10(b) operates to permit a law firm, under certain circumstances, to represent a person with interests directly adverse to those of a client represented by a lawyer who formerly was associated with the firm. The Rule applies regardless of when the formerly associated lawyer represented the client. However, the law firm may not represent a person with interests adverse to those of a present client of the firm, which would violate Rule 1.7. Moreover, the firm may not represent the person where the matter is the same or substantially related to that in which the formerly associated lawyer represented the client and any other lawyer currently in the firm has material information protected by Rules 1.6 and 1.9(c).

Rule 1.10(c) removes imputation with the informed consent of the affected client or former client under the conditions stated in Rule 1.7. The conditions stated in Rule 1.7 require the lawyer to determine that the representation is not prohibited by Rule 1.7(b) and that each affected client or former client has given informed consent to the representation, confirmed in writing. In some cases, the risk may be so severe that the conflict may not be cured by client consent. For a discussion of the effectiveness of client waivers of conflicts that might arise in the future, see Rule 1.7, Comment [22]. For a definition of informed consent, see Rule 1.0(e).

Where a lawyer has joined a private firm after having represented the government, imputation is governed by Rule 1.11(b) and (c), not this Rule. Under Rule 1.11(d), where a lawyer represents the government after having served clients in private practice, nongovernmental employment or in another government agency, former-client conflicts are not imputed to government lawyers associated with the individually disqualified lawyer.

Where a lawyer is prohibited from engaging in certain transactions under Rule 1.8, paragraph (k) of that Rule, and not this Rule, determines whether that prohibition also applies to other lawyers associated in a firm with the personally prohibited lawyer.